PEEK-A-BOO

Fraud Awareness, Prevention & Protection for #TEENS

Association of Certified Fraud Examiners

NATINA THALIEN - MBA, CFE
(Certified Fraud Examiner)

DEDICATION

Blayze, Savannah, Jade, Maxime, Keryann
Chase, Caitlin, Mitch, Zeke, Zadie, Victor,
Gabrielle, Jules, Nakayla, Natalie, Nicole, Chris,
Harlin, Kristi, Bill, Aaron, Teddy, Corinne,
Catherine, Patricia, Colette, Mélanie, Thiéry,
Frumènce and Bruno

To all of those teenagers who have struggled
with an injury, felt ashamed or depressed, suffer
from a disorder, been bullied, have anxiety, fight
addiction, had a broken heart, felt alone, been
abused, or been a victim of a fraud (scammed or
deceived); believe that change is possible. These
are all common problems and they are all
treatable.

In remembrance of Amanda Michelle Todd

In Recognition of

All adolescents who feel or have felt shocked,
panicked, powerless, afraid, unsafe, empty,
numb, or lonely; and are tired of hurting and
tired of feeling like no one understands what
they are going through.

SPONSORSHIP

Each book contributes to the Ritchie-Jennings Memorial Scholarship to the ACFE Foundation to support the education of students who have an interest in pursuing a career in Fraud Examination.

The scholarship provides an opportunity for students to advance their education and anti-fraud career path. Many of the students chosen for the scholarship go on to become Certified Fraud Examiners.
https://www.acfe.com/scholarship.aspx

A special thanks to Mr. Bruce Dorris, and the Leadership Staff of the Association of Certified Fraud Examiners!

Table of Contents

ACKNOWLEDGMENTS

This pocket guide is devoted to all teenagers aged 13 to 18 whose never-failing, unquestioned acceptance of the cosmic internet has encouraged me to write it. The point is not to stop using the internet completely or go hide in a corner or not have a connected device, but to just simply 'Be Aware'. It is to help you learn to identify and address vulnerabilities in your personal data and online habits; how to add additional protection to keep your data safe; what you should do in case your personal data does get stolen and you become the victim of a cybercrime. Many aspects of your life can remain online long after you have outgrown your connection with them. What is your internet footprint?[8] Become aware of what people can find out about you online; take steps to manage your image. The internet is only around 25 years old, so be mindful now, before you gain a - potentially adverse - online reputation; take control of it before years of information accumulates. We are all somewhat complex in many aspects of our lives; our personality changes as we grow in life. Today's rebel child is tomorrow's heart surgeon; even that secluded person who always sat alone could be running a giant corporation in the future. We can obtain certain things about someone's life through the prism of the internet, gaining some insight, but that might also display a skewed and inaccurate overall portrait. We can be eternally tied to one moment in time where we were caught on video or in a photo, whereby people draw an inaccurate or too broad conclusion about us for years to come. If this pocket guide can help just one person to think again before revealing too much about themselves on the internet, then all the time, energy, and research that went into this was well worth it.

The supercomputer known as 'Google' begins a relationship with you as soon as you start using it. It knows when you have family changes, who your boyfriend/girlfriend is, where you live, where you go to school, etc. It captures all kinds of information about you in a profile at http://www.google.com/settings/ads/. Google can see what pages you have searched on a website, how many times, how long you stayed on the website at http://tools.google.com/dlpage/gaoptout. Android with GPS locator 'On', stores your location history at https://maps.google.com/locationhistory. The history of your internet searches is tracked as well, logging every Google ad you ever clicked at https://www.google.com/history.

Your Account activity page also offers a list of all the apps that have any type of access to your data. You can see the exact type of permissions granted to the app, then revoke access to your data at https://security.google.com/settings /security/permissions. As Google owns YouTube, it tracks your searches https://www.youtube. com/feed/history/search_history. If minors are using 'Google Calendar' that, too, lets Google know where you are and at what time you will be there. Instead, use some private search engines that enable you to browse anonymously, such as DuckDuckGo, Qwant, Privatelee, WolframAlpha, Yippy, GIBIRU, Startpage, Hulbee, Disconnect Search, and Lukol.

It is said that no two 'snowflakes' are alike. The same applies to people; so, there can be no cookie-cutter solution for everybody. Do not take this pocket guide too literally but customize it to make the best use of whatever in it works for you. There are so many different scenarios from families and interpretations on how things ought to be in terms of minors on the internet, but there is no real definition that can explain things or no single perception that can visually be expressed. We all work from the same common denominator of just wanting our children to be happy, healthy, and educated with the right tools they need. At the very least, the "References & Resources" section can be of use one day for someone you know or love and care about or even for YOU, the reader.

A majority of my time is spent traveling *(>150 days a year)*, this allows me to experience many different places and meet various kinds of people. Sometimes, you cross paths with someone that is so intriguing that their acquaintance makes a difference in how you think about or see things. Francis Hounnongandji, Hugh Penri-Williams, and a specific colleague were huge professional influencers for me in ways of how they enthuse and engage the people around them to help plan for success. It has been truly those three individuals that continue to promote and encourage me to write and speak publicly to help prevent fraud, corruption, and misconduct amongst our generation that precedes us as well as to other Fraud Fighters. I would also like to thank Natalie for her input on this topic as both a mother and a teacher for children aged 10-11, where she is experienced in educating pupils who are in personally troubled environments or situations.

CHAPTER 1

INTRODUCTION

Not surprisingly, there are very few tools to teach the average internet user about the essential knowledge and awareness on how to reduce the dangers and be in control of your internet identity. The internet is something that is barely regulated and not directly policed. By accessing the internet, there are no rules, and therefore no rules to be enforced. We ALL voluntarily agree to send our personal sensitive information about ourselves to exchange for social interaction or to access a product, service, or retrieve information.

It is <u>not</u> so easy for a 'minor', as they are constantly juggling their emotional and rational feelings, all while trying to put everything in its place and be accepted and approved by everyone. This includes friends, teachers, parents, pastors, and coaches, and the more they give, the more that is asked of them. This pocketbook guide is to help provide explanations and resources around the clock, to make sure that the **HELP** required is tailored for the situation, no matter the gender, race, age, economic status, or location.

Minors seem more susceptible to fraud because they lack the human ability to judge the trustworthiness of people in general. Still naïve and un-experienced, they tend to believe what they see and hear. We are ALL sometimes guilty of this no matter our age, with even the smallest things we do in our daily lives. Even as adults, we are bombarded daily with requests to reveal our identities, if only for the business world to collect analytics to increase their sales.

For example, here are a few examples from our daily routines about how we are constantly bombarded with requests of who and where we are, and what we are buying.

Starbucks™ will personalize your coffee order by asking for your first name. This makes us feel 'good' to have someone call us by name, however, someone standing in line is a 'stalker/criminal/pedophile/rapist' who now knows your name and location to match all the 'Zadie's' in Paris, France. They know where you vacation, who your friends are, who your family is because they have found you on Facebook. It is easy to find someone and ALL their history (addresses, jobs, criminal records, etc.) just with a name, location, birthdate *(which Facebook gives if the settings are not properly secured)*. By the way, when posting photos on social media, talk about where you have **<u>been</u>**, not where you are!

You go to drive go-karts or golf with your family &/or friends, so you are asked for birthdate, full name, address *(obligation to sign-up before you drive/play)*. These requests sound as if you are were trying to get a bank loan, not just out for some recreational activity. Such types of questions with the associated exposure of our personal lives are being used to collect analytics for marketing purposes. It is not really needed, yet we continue to reveal personal information about ourselves, which can lead to the misuse of this data.

It is a very common practice in the USA for a waiter/waitress to walk away with a tray or credit card holder for your credit card and restaurant bill to process the payment. How do you know they do not take a photo of your card to use it later on for a purchase? Then they return with your credit card, receipt, and credit card voucher for you to sign, and leave a tip. If you did not use a pin code, then you need to sign. If you did use a pin code, then that replaces your signature. Payments are not processed the same way once you are outside the USA.

In Europe, for example in France, you will ask the server for your bill who will then come to your table with a handheld device *(called a countertop terminal, payment terminal, POS Point-of-Sale terminal, credit card terminal, EFTPOS-Electronic funds transfer at the point of sale or PDQ-Process Data Quickly terminal)* to process payment. They will not walk away with your card, nowadays they will rarely even touch your card, as you can just pay by placing your card close to their handheld device and payment is made. This is technically called "contactless payment", a secure method for customers to purchase products or services using a debit, credit, or smartcard, also known as a chip card, by using radio-frequency identification (RFID) technology or near-field communication (NFC).[10] To make a contactless payment, just hold your card near a terminal as explained above that is equipped with the contactless payment technology. As contactless payments do not require a signature or a personal identification number (PIN), transaction amounts are limited. This type of payment is most often how the French conduct purchases of no more than EUR 30 (increased to EUR 50 during Covid-19). The maximum authorized amount for a contactless transaction can vary by country/bank.

So, why is it so important not to let someone walk away with your credit card? It is not to say that EVERYONE is going to steal your card number. It is only to remind you to take precautions and realize that it is very, very easy to copy your credit card information to make online (internet) purchases with it later on. For example, the person who took a photo of your card can then make an online purchase, whether or not they use your card's CVV2 or verification code (3-

digits on the back of your credit card or 4-digits on the front for American Express) because certain websites do not require entering that code. This has been proven with several well-known internet sites by simply not always working on websites as you expect it to. It has been tested that just by creating or making up a phony CVV2, the transaction will still be accepted, even though the CVV2 is incorrect.

These are just a few examples of how ALL of us can open ourselves up to becoming victims of fraud. There are laws to protect minors and their privacy rights, called the *'Children's Online Privacy Protection Act* (COPPA)' which is a federal law in the USA that puts severe restrictions on what data companies can collect, share, or sell about children who are under the age of 13. A core provision under COPPA is that a website operator must obtain verifiable parental consent before any collection, use, or disclosure of personal information from children is used. However, it probably does not shock you to learn that minors are lying about their ages on social media!

A survey conducted by the Advertising Standards Authority researched what kind of ads young people see and whether companies follow the rules and codes for 'advertising'. It was discovered that more than 80% of minors lie about their age when using social media.[11] I must admit that I have friends and family whose profiles reflect someone who lives in places they have never been to, attended an Ivy League school with very impressive credentials, and celebrate different birthdays than the ones that I have shared with them many times before seeing their presence on social media. While this statistic is not shocking, I believe that profiles change once the individual starts to make their professional appearance in the world. Until the moment the individual does not take their profile seriously, they are completely exposed and share their bits and pieces of both real and fabricated virtual information. The survey found that 83% of the 11 to 15-year-olds whose internet usage was monitored were registered on a social media site with a false age. Just over 40% of the children who participated in the study were active social media users over 18 years of age, with one even claiming to be 88 years of age. This type of deliberate error causes advertisers to inaccurately target their ads to minors. The advertising can consist of gambling, alcohol, slimming aids, explicit sexual dating services, etc. This all stemmed from minors lying about their age, despite social media owners being well aware that young users are using false ages to log in, yet it remains a problem.

Advertisers and social media companies know that minors are falsifying their ages, hence there is heavy controversy on whose responsibility it is for the actions of the children doing so. The controversy is that the parents or legal guardian(s) are responsible for the child (minor) and their social media presence, yet the social media companies claim they cannot control the lies (falsified ages), likewise, advertisers do not claim responsibility because they are only targeting certain marketing segments based on a given profile.

When children lie about their age, it can

'cripple' their experience on the internet, because their values and intentions are distorted (not clear). It is important for schools, parents, safety organizations, guardians, pastors, friends, and family of all kinds to encourage children NOT to do this. Technology is being used to help identify children who have lied on the internet, but there is no substitute for action that can be taken by people who do know that particular child in the real world.

It **IS** true when you hear that information on the internet lasts forever. This is largely because of the existence of the internet archive. Perhaps you are reading this pocket guide because you have been victimized in some way, or perhaps it is just because your teacher has assigned it to you; either way – you should know that an internet archive exists. It is a non-profit organization that functions like a library (held in the state of California) and supports one of the largest known distributable digital media collections of photos, audio, and video files. They archive the internet at a certain moment in time and keep historical records of website content. This is known as the "Wayback Machine", which keeps searchable, linkable copies of internet sites that have existed in the past. If you want to know who was a school board member in 2003 or to search for a friend you once had contact with on a website that no longer exists, then they could probably be found at www.archive.org.[30]

My objective with this pocket guide is to provide the necessary information and tools to help prevent avoidable events by making you LESS LIKELY to become a victim, enabling you to protect yourself. If you have already been a victim of fraudulent activity, there is "HELP" for you in the TEEN Wellness chapter. Overall, increasing your knowledge makes you much more aware of the dangers posed by fraudsters and criminal masquerades that they perpetrate.

FRAUD & CORRUPTION

So, what is fraud? How does it differ from corruption? Generally, fraud is any dishonest activity causing actual or potential financial loss to any person or entity including theft of money or property whether or not by use of deception. It includes deliberate falsification, concealment, destruction or use of a falsified document, or improper use of information or position/status. The general elements of fraud include knowledge that the statement was false when uttered, and that it would cause loss to victim(s) damage. The victim relied on the false statement, so there were damages as a result.

Is <u>corruption</u> the same as <u>fraud</u>? The answer is 'no, it is not', but they are closely related. Corruption is the misuse of entrusted power for a private gain. It can be explained better with an example. Let us say Nicole and Savannah both sell widgets. Blayze is in the market for buying widgets and is comparing the widgets offered by Nicole and Savannah. Their widgets are both sold at EUR 50. However, Nicole decides to give a <u>personal</u>

<u>gift</u> to Blayze, if he buys her widgets. Nicole simply ***influenced*** Blayze's behavior, not done anything ostensibly wrong. However, Blayze has misused his power by accepting the widgets for his company and keeping the personal gift for himself. This is an example of corruption. The difference is that fraud requires deception, whereas corruption is a misuse of power. In even more simplistic terms, fraud is when you have cheated on a test/exam, while corruption can be illustrated by a pile of admission papers being reviewed with your paper being pulled out from the bottom because your mom has a friend that works in the administration office. Granted, this is a lite form of corruption, but you see how, if the advantage benefits you, that you then do not even consider it as corruption, perhaps just luck? Another example could be standing in a movie theatre line; suddenly several people from the back of the queue go through the side door because they know someone that works there. It is a misuse of power, and it comes in many different forms.

Numerous factors could cause a person to decide to steal, cheat, or lie: extreme financial pressure, psychological abnormalities, severe external pressures, hatred of financial institutions, or some other obsession. It is difficult to pinpoint an exact cause for any specific act of criminal or anti-social behavior. It is usually a combination of factors unique to that individual in their particular circumstance. One of the most critical points you should take away is the basic understanding that an individual's motivation for engaging in fraud or other types of deviant/unethical behavior is extremely complicated. However, searching for an explanation can be simplified using a professional theory called the Fraud Triangle. The Fraud Triangle helps us to understand why and how people commit fraud, but it is not a scientific theory and many times has been used in court, but the judge can reject it. It states that individuals are motivated to commit fraud when three elements come together: 1) some kind of perceived pressure 2) some perceived opportunity 3) some way to rationalize the fraud as not being inconsistent with one's values.

THE FRAUD TRIANGLE

A framework for spotting high-risk fraud situations

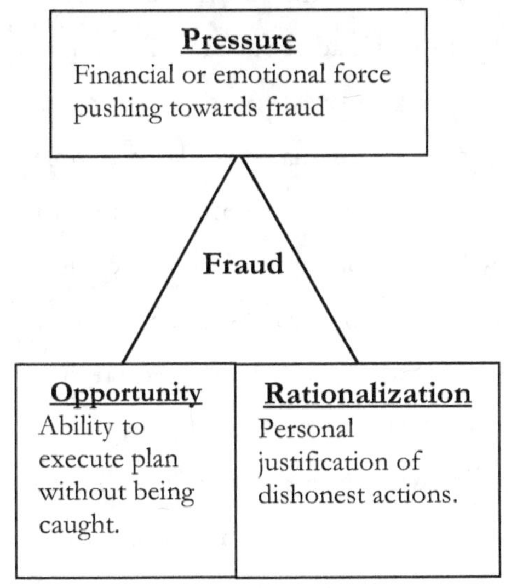

CHAPTER 2

TYPES OF FRAUD INVOLVING TEENS SOCIAL MEDIA PRESENCE

Social Media has become a platform to show the places you've traveled, the awards you've won, or the friendships you made or already had. While it is an amazing place to express one's individuality, it is argued that it leads to people feeling insecure, less than, or extremely envious of a person they know – or do not know, such as a stranger. The ones who debate social media say that it makes you take a step back when you realize how often people envy other people's lives and stop living their own because they are attached to their screen. All of those who participate on the internet exists in a world geared toward encouraging exposure of personal data. Social media sites are built to reward the sharing of information. The more people know you on Facebook, the more points of connection they find, and the more "friends' you will attract.

Social media refers to *websites and applications*

that are designed to allow people to create and share information, ideas, career interests, and other forms of expressions quickly, efficiently, and in real-time. The main advantage of social media, as opposed to traditional TV broadcasting, magazines, or newspapers, is that the quality, distance, frequency, interactivity, usability, timing, and performance are all improved than previously.

Previously, traditional digital media consisted of television, radio, newspapers, books, and magazines, and non-digital means of information fathering consisted of writing letters, phone calls (from a landline telephone), and face-to-face visits. Today, we can practically see the news live as it's happening by video calls via smartphones, drones, or satellites. The most popular social media websites include Facebook (Facebook Messenger), Instagram, WhatsApp, Google+, Myspace, LinkedIn, Pinterest, Snapchat, Tumblr, Twitter, Viber, VK, WeChat, Weibo, Baidu Tieba, TikTok, and Wikia.

There are said to be thirteen different types of social media, consisting of:

- o   Blogs
- o   Business Networks
- o   Collaborative Projects
- o   Enterprise Social Networks
- o   Forums
- o   Microblogs
- o   Photo Sharing
- o   Products/Services Review
- o   Social Bookmarking
- o   Social Gaming
- o   Social Networks
- o   Video Sharing
- o   Virtual Worlds

Minors are certainly familiar with one of these social media types. If they have a smartphone or tablet, then they are subject to mobile social media which refers to social media on such devices. Mobile social media is heavily used in marketing because there is a creation, exchange, and circulation of user-generated content, which assists companies with their marketing, research, communication, and relationship development.

It is important to understand the fundamentals of social media, and how they are working to understand the information that is being shared and its detrimental effects on minors if it is not used properly. The online world is full of chances to interact and share with others. It's also a place where nothing is temporary and there are no "take-backs." A lot of what <u>you do and say online</u> can be seen, even after you delete it - and it is a breeze for others to copy, screenshot, save and forward your information.

Facebook is the most widely used social network by individuals and businesses. It was initially started as a social network for students at Harvard (thefacebook.com) by Mark Zuckerberg *(who launched Facebook at age 20)* and later expanded to other colleges. In 2006, the Facebook network was opened to everyone over the age of thirteen and had an email address. According to terms of use of Facebook, it states that members must be at least 13 years old, and any member between the ages of 13 and 18 must be enrolled in school. Once you've created an account and answered some questions about where you work, live, and go to school, Facebook will activate a profile for you. In the fraud profession, investigators use social media searches to see registered public information such as names, email addresses, and phone numbers. All content on a social media site, no matter which one is being used will 'index; the content. Once something is indexed, it makes it searchable public information. You are probably thinking that you have your Facebook set to private, so you are just fine. However, I will explain to you how this misconception works so that you can better understand how it is possible to get your information with little to no effort. It is important to explain how social media works together to explain how your privacy settings are not always so private.

Facebook runs on a Google platform. Google's parent is Alphabet, Inc., which is a collection of companies running Google Maps, YouTube, Chrome, Android, WAZE, NEST, etc., while the other companies run as separate entities. Alphabet is a clever name because it covers many different activities from A–Z. This type of synergy allows Alphabet to have a huge management scale but allows businesses to run independently. Therefore, you think you are dealing with a specific company, but they are all inadvertently financially linked together under the same management, namely Alphabet. Since Facebook is on the Google platform, owned by Alphabet, the companies that Facebook bought are under this umbrella, too. In 2012, Facebook bought Instagram for USD1 billion from Mike Krieger & Kevin Systrom (both 28) who founded Instagram in 2010 with 13 employees, no revenues, and were only in the USA, Japan, and Brazil. In 2014, Facebook paid USD19 billion to Brian Acton (37) & Jan Koum (44) founders of WhatsApp, both ex-Yahoo employees, who had been denied jobs with Twitter and Facebook in previous years.

This is to demonstrate the idea that once you become attached to one application, the others are easily linked by the same monitoring and control methods. If you are private on the Facebook phone application and not private on your PC than your information is still exposed.

There are a couple of social media networks that are heavily used outside of the umbrella of Alphabet, which is Viber and Skype. Viber was developed by Viber Media and was founded in Tel Aviv, Israel by former Chief Information Officer (CIO) in the Israeli military, Talmon Marco, along with Igor Magazinnik, Sani Maroli, and Ofer Smocha. Viber was initially launched for iPhone on 2 December 2010, in direct competition with Skype. According to company data, 43.5% of Viber users are from the Middle East and Asia. In February 2014, a Japanese internet company bought Viber for USD900 million.

Skype was created by a Swede named Niklas Zennström and a Dane named Janus Friis. eBay acquired Skype Technologies for USD2.6 billion. This type of transaction made it easier for a pay-per-call basis using Skype. Skype made it easier for customers to pay for its fee-based services through PayPal, which is an online payment service, also owned by eBay.

Twitter was created in March 2006 by Jack Dorsey, Noah Glass, Biz Stone & Evan Williams, based in San Francisco, CA. It is a real-time information network that connects you to the latest information about what you find interesting. Twitter messages are public, but users can send private messages, it is also free and open to anyone. However, there are certain things to be aware of such as Twitter collecting personally identifiable information, sharing it with 3rd parties as they specify in their privacy policy. Twitter has the right to sell this information as an asset if the company changes hands. Twitter does not display advertisements, but advertisers can target users based on their history of tweets and could quote tweets in ads directed specifically at the user. Twitter is banned in Iran, China, North Korea, Egypt, Turkey, and Venezuela. Twitter has some interesting public facts that are shared on the internet such as:

- In April 2013, someone hacked the Associated Press Twitter account and tweeted that 2 bombs had exploded at the White House. The stock market crashed within seconds.

- Every tweet Americans send is being archived by the Library of Congress.

- The CIA (Central Intelligence Agency) reads up to 5 million tweets a day.

- A 2016 Twitter hack found that 123456 was the most common password, with more than 120,000 people using it.

- *'What is your password with Jimmy Kimmel Live'* is a good video to watch about password security practices https://www.youtube.com/watch?v=RJJEy GkS9jA. It demonstrates how passwords are not taken seriously. A good quote to remember is: "Treat your password like your toothbrush, do not let anyone else use it, and get a new one every six months." *Clifford Stoll: astronomer, author, first to utilize digital forensics successfully.*

SOCIAL MEDIA - FACEBOOK
#didyouknow?

Here are some notable points to share about Facebook, perhaps not commonly known.

- Exposure of personal life;

- Free and open to anyone;

- Facebook has privacy controls;

- Facebook does not share with the user who is looking at their profile;

- Access to listed friends, family, and colleagues.

- If you look at someone's profile often enough, Facebook assumes you are acquainted and starts to recommend you to that person (stalkers) – **CAREFUL!!** It is additionally possible that a recommendation could pop-up without ever going to look at another person's profile. This is a prime example of how big tech data is being used based on your browsing activity. For example, if Zeke and Aaron both play football at Viarmes High School in

Englewood, Indiana, and they both are looking at 'events' on Facebook; Facebook will recommend them to become friends.

- Facebook will pay YOU; between USD500 - USD10K if you find a 'bug' or can hack your way in; you've saved them the trouble of locating this, themselves.

- WhatsApp (which can also be used on your device) allows access to users' entire contact list, a valuable target for hackers. Status: continues to rely on open-sourcing to enable programs to fix bugs & improve security. The biggest criticisms from users are security, terrorism, and privacy.

- Any text that you put into the status update box is sent to Facebook's servers, even if you do not click the post button.
  #carefulwhatyoutype

- Over 600,000 hacking attempts that are made on Facebook accounts every day.
  #dontbeavictim

- Several people have been murdered for unfriending someone on Facebook

- Facebook tracks which site you visit, even AFTER you have signed out! *#clearyourbrowsersometimes*

- There are roughly 30 million dead people Facebook who still have 'live' profiles.

- It is estimated that 8.7% of Facebook users are fake. *#dontbenaive – online stranger contact*

- Facebook has a feature for you to designate who will manage your account after you die.

- Once something is posted or uploaded onto Facebook it becomes Facebook's property. So, if the original photographer uploaded the photo first onto Facebook and then others have taken it from there and uploaded it to their pages or profiles, this is legal and within their policy, and there is nothing that can be done about it.

- The average Facebook user in the USA spends 40 minutes a day on the site while checking their Facebook account 14 times on average. These statistics are for smartphone users only. In the UK, users spent an average of 58 hrs 39 mins each month browsing or using apps on smartphones, compared to 31 hrs 19 mins browsing on other devices.

Mark Zuckerberg will soon release a feature called: "Your Time on Facebook" for its Android app. It gives a tally of how much time a user spent on Facebook on their device during the last 7 days and the average time spent per day. A daily reminder can be set to alert the user when they have reached their assigned or self-imposed limit. There will also be a shortcut to change notifications settings. This screen time monitoring feature not only alerts the user but can even lock them out of their applications when they have exceeded their limit.

When you "Like" a photo on a public profile, your "Like" becomes searchable.

This is to show you that even if you are private, and you've 'liked' something public, then you have revealed yourself.

Facebook and Instagram started stripping out 'Exif data' from photos posted on Facebook. This is the information used to be able to search on a photo. However, you saw how Facebook is linked to all the others and how if someone "Likes" a photo, it can now be searchable.

Exif stands for Exchangeable Image File Format. It is the format that is used for storing metadata in an image and audio files. This includes digital photos, digital videos, etc. This feature is used in forensic investigations when you want to see all of the photo's information. Some sophisticated cameras and smartphones can attach geographic location data to photographs taken with them.   The camera can be identified (which iPhone it was), lens, exposure, flash, date, and location (latitude/longitude which will give us the location of the photo). When the user of the smartphone has their 'geo-location' settings on, which most of us do to run applications, etc.; then we can see this type of detail.

To give you an idea, as a Certified Fraud Examiner (CFE), we can take a pasted image (when a photo is copied & pasted) and look at false testimonials where they use the same face with different names. It can also be used to track

'Romance Scammers', as well as doing a reverse image search to see if someone has copied a house or apartment photo and then given several addresses for the same property. One of the special viewers we use is 'Jefferey's Image Metadata Viewer' at exif.regex.info for example.

ATTENTION!

The most common type of error is minors sending/receiving inappropriate photos. If you are a user who has taken a private photo and then afterward has deleted it from your phone; the photo is still available on the "server" of the Wi-Fi network server that you are using. It does not make a difference if it is free public Wi-Fi or your home photo; that photo is still there. It is no longer visible on your phone, but it still can be retrievable. Photos are run through an Exif Viewer, and then all information can be retrieved.

This type of activity is serious if you are under the age of 18, and there can be heavy consequences both personally and professionally *(photos can always resurface)*. The internet is forever. In many ways, that's amazing because there is access to information, articles, scandals, movies, and all sorts of other things, even if they happened decades ago. However, if you share an embarrassing photo, a questionable opinion, or a negative status update, it will stick around forever, even when you think it's gone.

If you are worried about your online reputation, start deleting right now. If you do not delete those inappropriate photos or not-so-nice opinions, someone will find them, and they will share them. When you gain any kind of 'fame' on the internet, people start researching you and try to find anything about you that is unfavorable to spread about you. Unfortunately, some people actually do this, and even more importantly the people that are entertained by it, but this pocket guide will help you to take control and keep control of 'You' in cyberspace by being less of a victim.

If you think that control of your personal data is broken, but you do not know what to do to fix it, or even worse to think you cannot do anything about it – please consider the following:

... But first – just relax, it is going to be okay!

Step 1: Update your software

The software on our devices gets out-of-date over time, and old software can contain security bugs or settings that leak personal data. It is important to make sure that your apps and operating systems are set to update automatically to ensure that you have the latest and safest versions installed.[12]

Step 2: Revisit your Privacy Settings

Update all of the privacy settings and afterward go into each of your application location settings, so that your location history is not leaking where it should not. Additionally, review the apps you have installed. If there are any you have not used for a while, remove them to reduce the chance of your data being shared.

Step 3: Download a Privacy browser on all your devices

The best-known browsers to use for privacy & security (meaning do not track your history, block ads, etc.) are Microsoft Edge, Opera, Chrome, Chromium, Safari, FreeNet, Vivaldi, Waterfox,

Brave, Tor Browser, Epic & Firefox. In my personal opinion, for the moment, I am a fond user of https://duckduckgo.com or https://www.qwant.com/?l=fr *(which is good to use, if you live in France)*. DuckDuckGo is a private alternative to Google Search: tracking is blocked, there are secure connections to websites, you can make private searches, and there is privacy for the websites that you visit (while on that website).[12]

Step 4: Manage your passwords

If your accounts are not secured, then your privacy is at risk. Most of us will use the same password on more than one website. When you do this, your privacy could be compromised due to data leaks. The best thing to do is to begin creating unique passwords for every website you use. This can be done by using a password manager. Password managers generate and store secure passwords for you automatically. Many browsers now have them built-in, or you can use independent tools such as Dashlane, LastPass, and 1Password, that can work across multiple browsers.

Step 5: Using two-factor authentication

Two-factor authentication is used in addition to your password, such as a code. This is another layer of protection and is best to use for all your major accounts. You can check if major sites have it available at https://twofactorauth.org/, which also links directly to the right documentation pages.

Teenagers tend to be pragmatic where they can follow or lead, be active or passive and be an independent, critical thinker, or a dependent, uncritical thinker – either way; they will be provoked or aggravated with fraud and they must possess the right tools on how to handle it.

A last note about Social Media is to tell you about a feature that Google offers called "Google Alert". This feature is used to know what 'someone' is saying online or what other people are saying about that 'someone'. Once you set-up a Google Alert, you will be notified whenever 'someone's' name appears online. If you want to set up a Google Alert, you need to www.google.com/alerts.

1. In the search terms box, type "someone's name" within quotation marks;
2. Select the type of alerts as "Comprehensive";
3. Select "How Often". If that "someone" is active online, "once a day" or "as it happens" might be the best choice;
4. Type in your e-mail address;
5. Click on the "Create Alert" button;
6. Go to your e-mail inbox, click on the link in the Google;
7. Alert e-mail to activate your alerts.

SEXUAL EXPLOITATION

It is a violation of federal law to knowingly send or attempt to send obscene material to a minor under the age of 16. If you have been SEXUALLY EXPLOITED online than you need to report this immediately at https://report.cybertip.org or call +1 800 THE LOST. This is the National Center for Missing & Exploited Children. They are the centralized reporting system for the online exploitation of children in the USA. It is a terrible feeling to feel like you are facing everything alone. Many people really do care for you and want to help, so please just reach out to them. They are already familiar with your situation and can give you solutions to help see you whatever it is you are faced with. It is a scary experience to have a sexually exploitative image of yourself exposed online. It can make you feel isolated and vulnerable, but there have been many others in the same situation as you, and they have overcome it. There is hope, please just extend your hand, there will be someone to take it and show you the way!

If you happened to have photos that you are not proud of there are some options to try and fix it. Firstly, perform a Google image search at www.images.google.com. The majority of the images that are displayed in Google's search results are from websites that are not owned by Google. Google is not the owner of the sites, so they do not remove images from the web. Therefore, best to contact the webmaster of the site, who can try and remove the page entirely. The idea is to go directly to the source of where the original photo is located.

This topic is discussed further in the section on CyberBullying in terms of photo-sharing on social media. Some photos exist on the internet that is easily accessed publicly.

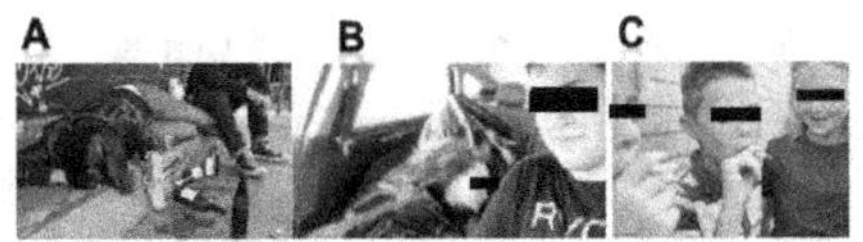

These sorts of photos cause social problems, as the persons who took these 'A' & 'B' photos cannot possibly be regarded as good friends. The publication of these photos shows that these minors could be at risk for possible physical problems such as weight gain, high blood pressure, cancer, liver disease, hangovers, low immunity, heart and lung failure, even alcohol poisoning. Abusing alcohol can also lead to unwanted, unplanned, and unprotected sexual activity; even physical or sexual assault. Additional problems to consider could also be school problems, legal problems, alcohol-related car crashes, and other unintentional injuries, even death from alcohol poisoning.

Furthermore, it is possible to see on Facebook which individuals 'liked' these posted photos by going to the Facebook page, and right-click on the photo. Copy the link, paste it somewhere, take the unique ID number from the photo, then go to www.graphs.tips/Facebook and type the number into the fields. It will show you all the 'posts' that the individual liked or other posts they had made.

According to a study, 1 in 3 people feel more dissatisfied with their lives after visiting Facebook.

The top 10 reasons noted for using Facebook were:

1. Cannot remember birthdays
2. People want to read the news
3. Feel as though a 'duty' to like something & post something
4. Attention Seekers
5. Watch people secretly
6. Boredom
7. Need Facebook to promote their work
8. Support a Social Cause, or Track Events
9. Remain connected with Friends (memories from school) & Family
10. Suffer from 'FAD' – Facebook Addiction Disorder *(cannot resist)*

Continue to enjoy social media, but BE AWARE of the potential crimes involved, so that you minimize your risk of becoming a victim. The 7 most common Facebook crimes are:

1. Scams
2. CyberBullying
3. Stalking
4. Robbery

5.   Identity Theft

6.   Defamation

7.   Harassment

Defamation is when someone communicates a false statement in writing that harms the reputation of a person, business, product, group, government, religion, or country.

When fraud is committed to someone it can cause emotional and psychological devastation that damages the victims such as insomnia, persistent feelings of anxiety, embarrassment and shame, loss of appetite, ongoing anger and resentment, depression, and suicidal thoughts. This pocket guide is to encourage victims to seek help so that they report or communicate such activity and do not remain in constant anxiety and unhappiness.

ONLINE GAMING
(Video Games)

There seem to be many online multiplayer shooting games that have been accused of being both addicting and enjoyable. Some believe that certain games are hyped up and will eventually die down, and others have classified certain video games as a "Gaming Disorder".

Whether you believe that online games create violent aggression or oppression or whether you believe gaming provides social life skills, teamwork, enhanced memory, problem-solving, and coordination improvement, be mindful of certain Cybersecurity precautions. Each family has its own set of boundaries and opinions about what is appropriate for their children. If there is resistance in a household due to certain games being played, then parental judgment and the age restrictions of the game are the priority. If a parent or legal guardian is not aware of the game, they are encouraged to educate themselves about it before taking any decision and perhaps even watch, play and converse with the minor about it. With any luck, this fad will pass (*as it usually does*). Keep in mind that game designers know how to captivate an audience and how to hook players to keep them coming back for more. Players get an adrenaline rush by getting that 'near miss' phenomenon making them feel like they have almost won, which keeps them coming back for more. Players should positively set some limits so that their involvement includes playing yet still having time to do real-world things. Players should be fair with themselves and find their balance, as their time as a minor is only a small portion of their entire life. They will spend the majority of their life as an adult, so they should try and spend time with their true friends and family.

However, if this is too light for you, and there could be a serious online gaming problem, there is help available. Firstly, there are several addiction symptoms to watch out for:

- Being irritable or moody when they cannot play.

- Lack of control over gaming. They play because they cannot stop.

- Losing interest in other activities, e.g. sports, exercise.

- Constantly needing to play more and more ("it's never enough").

- Being deceptive, e.g. stealing money to buy things inside the game.

- Increased Anxiety or Depression.

- Jeopardizing school, work, and/or relationships

- Ignoring serious health issues due to marathon gaming, such as:[13]

❖ *Deep Vein Thrombosis* is a condition caused by frequently sitting still for too long and this can cause life-threatening blood clots. This has been known to happen to players who went on vacation and spent four days straight on a PlayStation, or to another individual who participated in a 12-hour gaming session. These individuals were rushed to the hospital because they had developed blood clots in their legs. Tragically, the one who played the 12-hour gaming session died from Thrombosis, the other did live, but certainly changed his gaming habits.

❖ *Cardiac failure* can occur when you continuously stay awake for a certain amount of days, which can put an extreme strain on your body; especially if you are in poor health already, it can prove too much pressure for your heart.

❖ *Nintendonitis* is a condition that happens when you repeatedly perform the same motion over and over. Even if a player does take breaks and keeps their body active between gaming sessions, the repetition of using a controller for hours, days, weeks, months, and years on end can still take an enormous toll on their body. Gaming typically requires a lot of repetitive motions with your thumbs & fingers.

❖ *Lower back pain* has been connected to gaming by research performed by the European Spine Journal. So, if you must play, at least fix your posture.

❖ Computer Vision Syndrome (CVS) is a condition that affects those who spend several hours looking at screens *(including but not limited to TVs, computers, smartphones, or tablets)*. It can cause a wide range of problems, most commonly led by eye strain and eye pain. These problems can be aggravated by low light and bad posture. If you are someone who binges in marathon gaming sessions and cannot be convinced otherwise based on the previously noted health issues, at least make sure you have an appropriate chair and good lighting.

The key difference between when a game turns from a hobby into a gaming problem for someone is when it creates a negative impact on their current life - repeatedly. If online gaming is causing problems, and they continue to play out despite the negative impact it is causing them, then it is recommended to seek the help of a professional when all other avenues have been exhausted. Some remedies can help to limit young people's involvement with video games, such as completing homework beforehand, being physically active in sports, participating in family life, getting enough sleep before playing.

Here is some addiction support shared by Game Quitters who recommend certain best practices for excessive online gamers.[9]

- Two hours or less of gaming time perhaps not every day;

- Require homework & exercise to be completed first;

- Remove gaming devices from the bedroom *(centralize)*;

- Maintain firm, strong, consistent boundaries;

- No technical devices at the dinner table or during car rides;

- Devices handed to a parent/guardian one hour *(or more)* before bedtime;

- Maintain other hobbies & interests;

- No gaming first thing in the morning;

- Maintain real-life friends and face-to-face interactions.

Aside from gaming addiction, cyberbullying is another significant social issue, as the invisibility of online interaction can lead children to utilize less self-control and behave in ways that they would not 'offline'. Many children and teens report being bullied in some way online. Oftentimes, adults are unaware that a minor (related or unrelated) is a victim of cyberbullying? This is unfortunate as cyberbullying leads to significant long-lasting negative effects such as anxiety, depression, increased stress, suicidal thoughts, or actions. Protective factors against cyberbullying while gaming includes consistent adult monitoring of internet usage, boundaries on time spent on the internet and content consumed.

Here are more tips to help 'Gamers' when they are online:

- Know that everyone is a stranger. If a friend invites you to game online, have him/her call/text you to verify that they are really your friend.

- Ensure that your devices are up to date with the latest versions of firewall, antivirus & antispyware software.

- Create a safe zone at home! TEENS must know that parents will not take away their privileges or stop them from playing, if they come and share a situation with a parent or guardian that makes them uncomfortable or if they have questions.

- Take the time to play! It is possible to pre-screen all your kid's games before they are allowed to play them. If you are a parent/guardian, you could watch the 'demo' or ask them to play a session with you to get an idea of how it works. It would be ideal if parents/guardians and TEENS periodically played their games together.

- Take a look at your account name for the game. An e-mail account name should never by a minors' nickname or identify them as a young boy or girl since gaming names should not give away personal information. If you are a 13-year-old girl, and your account name is "Hottie", this should be fixed by a change, otherwise, it conveys the impression of being easy and available to boys or online stalkers. Although a young girl might find the attention amusing, it could invite a dangerous interaction between a young flattered innocent girl with someone who is a cybercriminal or cyberstalker. Parents and guardians should know the account names of their kids and what type of content is being streamed. Information about which games are most appropriate for your family can be referenced through the Entertainment Software Rating Board at https://www.esrb.org/. The ESRB ratings provide information about what a game or app contains in terms of rating categories, content descriptions, and interactive elements for the consumer to make informed choices. If you are a teen and you find the live stream conversation improper or vulgar – excuse yourself and leave the game.[14]

- If the Gaming rooms have many people that you do not know in the 'room', then you should **block** the text and voice chat on the games.

CHAPTER 3

CYBERCRIME
WEBCAM HACKING

What is a webcam? A webcam is simply an electronic camera connected to a device either wirelessly (Wi-Fi) or directly; it records images to be displayed elsewhere. Webcams are used by all sorts of people and for sorts of all different reasons. They are often intended for personal use in the home by people who want to give distant visual access to someone else. Can also be used for security measures to see or monitor what goes on in a specific location. For example, you can have a camera in your home and monitor the activity while you are at work, on vacation, while children are at school or day-care, or just to see what your pet is doing all day. Webcams are also used to video conference for business purposes. The different uses of a webcam are endless; webcams are wonderful for overcoming distances. Webcams vary a lot in their capabilities & features, reflected in the price. Some webcams capture a still image only once every 30 seconds, while others provide a streaming video of 30 images per second.

Webcam hacking is a process by which one person takes over someone else's webcam. Hacking a webcam is where someone has discovered a way to hack into a remote webcam and watch them. If you use a camera connected to the web, someone could be watching you! Any electronic device connected to the internet can be infiltrated: desktop/laptop computers, tablets, security cameras, smartphones, and much more. Attacks do not even have to focus on the equipment supporting the webcam. Hackers can enter home networks through any unsecured or lightly secured entry point on the network. The boom in internet devices has created a universe of vulnerable entry points into home networks. An overwhelming number of manufacturers implement only basic passcodes on devices, sometimes as simple as 123456. In some cases, devices are not protected with codes at all. If the devices do have some level of security, they do not update the security settings as often as other device manufacturers do. Most people are not aware when someone seizes outside control of their device. Unfortunately, women are statistically more frequently targeted by hackers for various reasons, including spying and profit. Some hackers focus on both purposes simultaneously.

One of the most high-profile webcam hacking incidents in the USA involved the *2013 Miss Teen USA*, Cassidy Wolf. A former classmate silently watched her through the webcam of the computer in her bedroom. He eventually emailed photos to her, threatening to release them to the public, if she did not undress for him in front of the camera. She contacted the police, then immediately filed a complaint with the FBI, who prosecuted the hacker. The court sentenced him to 18 months in prison for the crime. The CNN interview with Cassidy Wolf can be seen at https://www.youtube.com/watch?time_continue=78&v=8fQieCMoym0.

There are many approaches that hackers take

to try and enter the lives of their targets, whether they are down the street or across the world. The main approach is through email messages that claim to offer information or entertainment to readers. Users click on the files attached to the messages or click on links embedded in the correspondence to access the information. The technical term for this type of technique is called 'phishing'. Another example involves luring email recipients to visit a website that hackers know is of great interest to their victim. Once the victim goes to the website, the website actually downloads malware onto the viewer's machine. The user just follows the sender's instructions, unwittingly downloading malware onto their device. In many instances, they allow a RAT (Remote Access Trojan) into their systems. These viruses are particularly invasive forms of malware that can give a hacker complete, unrestricted control of a device.

What to do to Prevent Webcam Hackers?

It does not make a big difference whether you are using a Mac or PC, just ensure that you are always running the latest anti-virus and other security software on your device. Suitable software will do most of the work to detect and block all kinds of malware. The second helpful tip is to make sure that you have your firewall turned on. Devices connected to a home network should already be protected by a firewall that monitors network traffic, blocking unrequested incoming connections. Make sure your firewall is turned on!

For Windows 10, click the Windows logo in the bottom left corner of the screen, then the Settings 'wheel' followed by Update & Security - Windows Security - Firewall & network protection: then activate Domain network - Private network - Public network, as appropriate.

For MacOS, go to System Preferences, Security & Privacy, choose Firewall, click Turn On Firewall (NB you need Admin Access capability to do this!).

Also, keep your software patches updated, be cautious about opening email attachments and clicking on potentially dangerous links. If you have an internet-accessible camera elsewhere in your house – including baby monitors, be aware that many such devices are sold with default or weak passwords that are very easy for hackers to crack. Make sure to configure them with unique, hard-to-guess passwords. Similarly, you should update your webcam's firmware regularly to protect against newly discovered security holes and vulnerabilities. Remember to secure your Wi-Fi connection by frequently changing the router's default password by creating a powerful and unique password to make it harder to decrypt.

Hackers lure people into downloading and installing RAT software using email attachments, pictures, and links. Use caution before opening emails from people you do not know, never open attachments from an unknown sender, and do not click a link within an email. Instead, hover over it to see the full URL in the lower corner of your browser: if the URLs do not match, do NOT click the link. Also, use caution before clicking on shortened links or quick access links on social media as they can be corrupted *(corrupted means containing errors or alterations)*.[15] Lastly, avoid tech support offers, where hackers might contact you by saying there are some problems with your device. They will try and convince you to download a remote-access software that will allow them to fix those alleged problems. Do not trust anyone who contacts you offering this kind of support. Consider disabling both Windows Remote Assistance and Remote Desktop as those are other methods for hackers to gain remote access to your device.

Furthermore, although it can be misleading in some cases, see if your webcam's LED lights up unexpectedly. It could imply unauthorized access: control by a hacker or by a peeper.

Cover your webcam *(place a piece of tape over it or bandaid)*, deactivate in Preferences, or just unplug, if external. If you only use your webcam infrequently, then just put a sliding cover or a Post-it note over your lens, so you can choose when you want to be "on camera" and when not.

Today, many businesses are selling 'scanners', i.e. software that analyses your home network, makes a list of all connected devices, thereby revealing common cybersecurity vulnerabilities. The internet does provide an abundance of information and it does bring people together, but at the same time, consumers need to focus on how they are potentially being exposed. Consider strong internet security and practice extreme alertness!

Ideally, there is not a best-defined solution that consumers can rely on for security. Companies continue to create devices or programs that will give quicker, more efficient results, but they do not take accurate measures to protect all of our devices and thereby our identity.

CYBERSECURITY

What is Cybersecurity? Cybersecurity concerns the protection of internet-connected systems, including hardware, software & data from cyber-attacks. 'Security' consists of both cybersecurity & physical security, which is to protect against unauthorized access to your data, information, and other computerized systems. It secures confidentiality, integrity & availability of your data. To put it more informally: information security involves securing data in any form, e.g. locking paper documents in a filing cabinet, file storage rooms, or storing electronic data on IT devices, whereas cybersecurity concentrates on protecting data held electronically.

Cybersecurity is a problematic element for minors because of the constantly evolving nature of security risks. Technology & application providers do not protect minors against the most known threats, leaving minors completely undefended. Recently, The National Institute of Standards & Technology issued updated guidelines (voluntary cybersecurity framework) in its risk assessment framework that recommends a shift toward continuous monitoring and real-time assessments, but only certain industries have adopted such an approach.

The process of following new technologies, concerning security trends and data intelligence, is a challenging effort. However, it is necessary to protect information and other assets from cyber threats, which take many forms, such as:

<u>Ransomware</u> is a type of malware (malicious software) that involves an attacker locking the victim's device's system files - typically through encryption - and demanding a payment to decrypt and unlock them.

<u>Malware</u> is malicious software, or any file or program used to harm a device user, such as worms, viruses, Trojan horses & spyware. Trojan horse is a malicious program *(a program, such as a game or a link, that appears friendly, but that contains applications destructive to the device's system)* designed to appear like a legitimate program; once activated following installation, Trojans can execute their

malicious functions. This is what happens when your device *crashes*. If your device is infected by malware, it could be exhibiting one or more of these symptoms:[16]

- Your device is running very slowly.

- You receive alarming pop-up messages while surfing the internet, claiming that you need to download software to get rid of it or update it to a new version.

- Your antivirus & firewall protections have been disabled automatically.

- Unfamiliar and special error messages indicating that your programs will not run, or your files will not open.

- Hardware such as USB keys & printers no longer respond to commands.

- File sizes fluctuate, even when you are not accessing those files.

Social engineering is an attack that relies on human interaction to trick users into breaking security procedures to gain sensitive information that is typically protected.

Phishing is a form of fraud where fraudulent

emails are sent that resemble emails from reputable sources; however, these emails intend to steal sensitive data, such as credit card &/or login information.

CYBERBULLYING

CyberBullying is emotionally devastating to both the victim and their families. It is not something to be tolerated and there are actions that you can take, both as parents and victims. You are not alone, there is 'Help' for you in all forms who are waiting for you to reach out to them which is noted in the **Teen Wellness** section of this pocket guide.

Generally, incidents of bullying are not a one-time thing.[4] Bullies target the same person or group over and over again. Those who engage in bully-like behaviors use their strength, popularity, or power to harm, control, or manipulate others. They will usually target those who are weaker in size might have a difficult time defending themselves. The statistics on bullying reveal that it is spiraling out of control and is an increasing problem with minors. Cyberbullying is a form of 'harassment'. Harassment is a behavior that seeks to make a person feel intimidated or threatened, or that creates a generally hostile environment for someone in a particular place.[4]

What is CyberBullying? It is using social media, e-mail, chat rooms, websites, and other forms of electronic communication to:

- Send mean-spirited messages;
- Make cruel and harmful remarks about individuals;
- Post unflattering or derogatory photos;
- Make direct threats or encourage acts of violence;
- Sexual Harassment;

Cyberbullying is sometimes easy to spot and sometimes it is less obvious, like impersonating a victim online or posting personal information, video, or photo of someone which is *intentionally* designed to hurt or embarrass another person. **Note:** It is a crime to impersonate another person if harm is caused.[17] False impersonation occurs when someone represents themselves as another person to deceive others. However, the key element of this offense in most cases is whether an additional act was performed, beyond the deceitful misrepresentation, that: creates a legal or financial liability for the person being impersonated; or benefits the impersonator.

False impersonation is a serious offense, and a prosecutor's decision as to whether the charge would be a misdemeanor or felony rests on the circumstances of the case, and the accused's criminal history. As a misdemeanor offense, a conviction brings the potential for summary probation, one year in county jail, and USD10,000 in fines, while a felony conviction brings up to three years in jail, USD10,000 in fines, and/or formal probation.[17] Further, anyone convicted of the felony charge of false impersonation is prohibited from owning firearms.

In general, there are many ways that someone can fall victim to or experience cyberbullying when they are using technology and the internet. The most common methods of cyberbullying today are:

Harassment – When someone is being harassed online, they are being subjected to a string of abusive messages or efforts to contact them by one person or a group of people. People can be harassed through social media as well as through their smartphone (texting and calling) and email. The majority of communication that the victim will receive is malicious or threatening.

Doxing – Doxing is when an individual or group of people distribute, another person's personal information such as their home address, smartphone number, or place of work onto social media or public forums without that person's permission to do so. <u>Doxing</u> can cause the victim to feel extremely anxious and it can affect their mental well-being.[1]

Cyberstalking – Cyberstalking is similar to harassment and involves the perpetrator making persistent efforts to gain contact with the victim, however, this differs from harassment – more commonly than not, people will cyberstalk another person due to deep feelings towards that person, whether they are positive or negative. Someone who is cyberstalking is more reluctant to eventually escalate their stalking off of the internet as well.

Revenge porn – Revenge porn, is when

sexually explicit or compromising images of a person have been distributed onto social media or shared on revenge porn specific websites without their permission to do so. Normally, images of this nature are posted by an ex-partner, who does it to cause humiliation and damage to the reputation of their ex-partner. This crime has increased immensely around the globe and now there are revenge porn laws. England and Wales passed the Criminal Justice and Courts Bill that includes an amendment to address revenge porn. If you are convicted of trafficking in revenge porn in these countries, you could face up to two years in prison. Several U.S.A States have revenge porn prohibition statues as well. This demonstrates that social media networks are beginning to stand up for revenge porn victims. Since 2015, Twitter will now immediately remove any "link to a photograph, video, or digital image of you in a state of nudity or engaged in any act of sexual conduct." That has been posted without consent. Google will also delete these images upon request, and Microsoft created an online form for victims to fill out to request removal of revenge porn as well. If you are a victim, there are Revenge Porn Lawyers who are available and have extensive experience working with traumatized people. There are resources available to victims and those are noted in the TEEN Wellness & Outreach section of this pocket guide.

Swatting – Swatting is when someone calls emergency responders with claims of dangerous events taking place at a specific address.[18] People swat others by intending to cause panic and fear when armed response units arrive at their home or place of work. Swatting is more common within the online gaming and streaming community and is a form of payback following an online dispute. The process consists of the attacker finding their target's home address, and then they proceed to make the swatting call to the victim's local police department with the intent to cause a large police response. The details of the call will vary from call to call, but typically, the 'swatter' will often claim that someone has been seriously injured or a hostage situation is taking place. It is common for the swatter to claim that the victim is armed, and this raises the urgency to a potentially life-threatening situation for the responding police officers. Now, there is an added risk for the victim's safety as both the victim and the police are both taken by surprise.

There was one particular incident where such a phone call resulted in death because the swatter said that the victim had killed his father, was holding his mother and sibling at gunpoint, and had doused the house in gasoline. This was a fabricated story by the swatter and had turned violent, due to 'swatting'.[18]

Corporate attacks – In the corporate world, attacks can be used to send masses of information to a website (Dedicated Denial-of-Service) in order to take the website down, causing it to cease to function. Such corporate attacks can seriously affect public confidence, damage business reputations, and, in some instances, force the business to fail.

Account hacking – Cyberbullies can hack into a victim's social media accounts and post abusive or damaging messages. This can be particularly damaging for brands and public figures.

False profiles – Fake social media accounts can be set up to damage a person or a brand's reputation. This can easily be done by obtaining publicly available images of the victim and making the account appear as authentic as possible.

Slut-shaming – Slut-shaming is when someone is called out and labeled as a "slut" for something that they have done previously or even just how they dress. This kind of cyberbullying often occurs when someone has been sexting another person and their images or conversations become public. Sexting is sending, receiving, or forwarding sexually explicit messages, photographs, or images, primarily between smartphone, of oneself to others. It is seen more commonly within young people and teenagers, but anyone can fall victim to being slut-shamed.

Fat-shaming / Body-Shaming – Fat Shaming is a term that is used to refer to the act of making fun of obese people or people who are overweight.[19] It can also mean the act of harassing fat or obese people. Body Shaming is similar to fat-shaming as it is the act or practice of humiliating a person based on their body type in general by making critical and/or unkind/rude statements about their body shape and size.[22]

We live in a society where appearance can be used to judge a person before words are even exchanged.[21] The importance of appearance seems to date back since the beginning of time, but advertisements, newspapers, billboards, print ads, movies, music videos, shopping windows, etc. help to portray a certain image in society both online and in-person, which has created a pattern for certain behavior. A stylish and clean individual indeed gives a different first impression than a sloppy and dirty one, but the size of an individual whether they be too fat, too skinny, too tall, too short or any other 'shaming' of weight or appearance is a negative judgment and depending to what extent – considered bullying. It is already so difficult to be a teenager; it is a constant battle to keep a positive outlook for self-esteem and confidence. It is important to remember that, every single person you know would change something about them physically if they could. This is an endless, vicious circle throughout a person's life. One-minute, physical appearance becomes an understanding of 'mental' health and wellness. That your inner self-worth is more precious than your outer beauty. This is certainly a lot easier said than done, but it takes a deep understanding of that concept until you can cross over and take charge of 'You', and not be influenced so much by others' opinions about your appearance or weight. If your appearance is based on hygiene, well, that is simply a matter of education or being rebellious. However, if you are a victim of fat-shaming or body-shaming then perhaps theses points could help you focus:

- Do not put your primary focus on weight

and outer beauty; seek a healthy lifestyle that works best for you.

- Limit your social media usage; tell the person who is bullying you to stop or step-in if you see others being bullied. If the person does not stop, talk to an adult about it, or skip to the Teen Wellness chapter and use the hotline number.

- Look up to realistic and inspiring every-day heroes. There are so many wonderful and inspirational people in the world who all have different weights, sizes, and looks.

- Have compassion and appreciation for your classmates who struggle with their weight or body. It could be health-related, or a constant battle for that individual. If you are the victim who is being 'shamed', remember that even the person who is doing the bullying is probably also suffering from their very own imperfections as well.

REPORTING THE WRONGDOER

Cyberbullying cannot always be constituted as accidental when the impersonal nature of the text message, email, or IM (instant messaging) makes it difficult to detect the sender's tone. That is to say, one person's joke could be insulting and/or hurtful to another. However, a repeated pattern of texts, emails, and online posts is hardly misconstruable as accidental. By nature, we are taught that it is not good to be a 'Tattle-Tale'. It is a personal dilemma when we are faced with a decision to report a wrongdoer. No one wants to isolate themselves from the group by snitching on their friends. However, there is also that underlying thought that if we remain silent then there is a risk that someone could get hurt (either emotionally or physically).

Minors are reluctant to report being bullied, even to their parents, and although there are surveyed statistics; it is impossible to know just how many are affected. The Centers for Disease Control and Prevention (CDC) have performed recent studies where they've taken Global Schools and provided the student with Health surveys. There are various statistics from a Risk Behavior Survey under 'unintentional injuries and violence' between male and female students at https://www.cdc.gov that parents might want to be aware of. These statistics were based on a survey given to students with questions asking students if they were:

- Were threatened or injured with a weapon on school property?

- Were in a physical fight?

- Were in a physical fight on school property?

- Were electronically bullied? *(Cyberbullying)*

- Were bullied on school property?

- Did not go to school because they felt unsafe at school or on their trip to/ from school?

- Felt sad or hopeless? *(Depression)*

- Made a plan about how they would attempt suicide? *(this was 41.1% in females & 21.4% in males)*

- Attempted suicide?

- Suicide attempt resulted in an injury, poisoning, or overdose that had to be treated by a doctor or a nurse?

Cyberbullying rates have found that about 1 in 4 teens have been the victims of cyberbullying; about 1 in 6 admit to having cyberbullied someone. There were certain studies in locations surveyed where *more than half of the teens* surveyed said that they have experienced abuse through social and digital media.

The following are just a few examples of how cyberbullying can surface with minors:

A clique of junior high school girls having a sleepover pretend to befriend an unpopular girl on Instant Messenger (Facebook). They persuade her to reveal her deepest/private feelings, secrets, and obsessions. The next day at school they show everyone the conversation, and she is mortified. **#betrayel**

Harlin, a high school junior, secretly takes a smartphone photo of Maxime, an over-weight kid, who is undressing in the gym locker room. Within minutes, the photo is sent to Harlin's friends in Spanish class. When Maxime finds out, he is so embarrassed that he refuses to return to school. **#breachofprivacy**

Caitlin is a 16-year-old who has created a Web Blog all about herself. An anonymous person starts posting threatening sexual comments with links to porn websites on her blog. **#postings**

One of the most radical cases due to cyberbullying *(cybercide)* began with 15-year-old Canadian student Amanda Michelle Todd's tragedy *(27 November 1996 – 10 October 2012)*. Amanda was a chronic victim of cyberbullying who committed suicide by hanging herself at her home in the province of British Colombia, Canada. Before her death, Amanda posted a 9-minute video on YouTube in which she used a series of flashcards to tell her experience of being blackmailed into exposing her breasts via webcam, of being bullied and physically assaulted. Amanda's video went viral after her death, resulting in international attention from the media. The video had more than 12 million views as of August 2018. This tragedy started national discussions on criminalizing cyberbullying. Amanda's mother, Carol Todd, created a program against cyberbullies after her death. Studies of the scope and severity of bullying have spread internationally. Currently, funding and support for anti-bullying organizations are established; useful resources are provided in detail in the TEEN Wellness chapter of this pocket guide. There are national, state, and local help facilities, centers, clinics, camps, hotlines available for minors internationally. You are not alone, there are people available as experts who can help find a solution.

#call-for-help

Facebook's security unit investigated Amanda's case and forwarded their report to the USA authorities' Child Exploitation & Online Protection Center, onward to the British National Crime Agency, then to the Dutch authorities. In January 2014, the Dutch police arrested a 35-year-old man involved where they found multiple victims in the Netherlands, UK, and Canada. He had installed spyware on their devices with very disturbing chat logs of extortion, numerous images of child pornography, 5,800 bookmarked names of potential victims, and their social networks. The 35-year-old man, known as Aydin Coban in the Netherlands, of Dutch and Turkish citizenship, had been charged with indecent assault and child pornography, extortion, internet luring, criminal harassment, possession, and distribution of child pornography for his alleged offenses against Amanda and other child victims, both male and female. On 16 March 2017, he faced 72 charges of sexual assault and extortion in the Netherlands involving 39 alleged victims (34 young women, 5 men) in various countries such as the USA, Norway, the UK, and Canada. Several individuals had been harassed for years. He faces Dutch and Canadian sentences of 10 years and 8 months.

There are thousands of cases of suicide due to bullied minors, which has created a new term called 'BullyCide'. The hybrid term, BullyCide, is referred to as suicide caused by the results of bullying. Minors who are bullied live in a constant state of fear and confusion in their lives. It is a profound feeling that they cannot escape the rumors, insults, verbal abuse, and terror; so, they feel as though their only solution is to take their own life. BullyCide is a repulsive and serious issue that parents, teachers, caretakers, and authorities face today.

Several different reasons could ultimately lead to BullyCide, including:

- Alone (friendless) bullied victims without any support or encouragement while being bullied regularly;

- Continuous bullying either emotionally or physically;

- Non-stop emotional & physical pain;

- Constantly being tormented or continually harassed from a most embarrassing moment, that is too heavy for them to carry or live with;

- Victim of being bullied by an authority figure like a parent, teacher, coach, pastor, neighbor, or another adult.

- It is statistically noted that many times the

victims are known to their predators, and trusted by the parents; making it difficult for them to come forward.

Amanda Todd's YouTube video used 74 note cards to detail the severe mental distress she endured from classmates and strangers in the consequence of a revealing (topless) screenshot chat photo wrongfully exposed to her Facebook friends and others by an extortionist stranger. Amanda's video does not have any sound, but the following post-it notes were displayed four hours before her death.

Hello!
I've decided to tell you about my never-ending story
In 7th grade, I would go with friends on webcam
Meet and talk to new people
Then got called stunning, beautiful, perfect, etc. …
Then wanted me to flash
So I did…. 1-year later….
I got a msg on Facebook
From him…. don't know how he knew me.
It said… if you don't put on a show for me I will
send The boobs
He knew my address, school, relatives, friends, family
names,
Christmas break….
Knock at my door at 4 am.
It was the police… my photo was sent to everyone

I then got really sick, and got…
Anxiety, major depression, and panic disorder
I then moved and got into Drugs + Alcohol
My anxiety got worse… couldn't go out
A year past and the guy came back with my new
List of friends from school, But made a Facebook
page
My boobs were his profile pic.
Cried every night, and lost my friends and respect
People had for me… again…
Then nobody liked me
Name-calling, judged…
I can never get that photo back
It's out there forever…
I started cutting…
I promised myself never again
Didn't have any friends and I sat at lunch alone
So I moved schools again
Everything was better even though I still sat alone
At lunch in the library every day
After a month later I started talking to an old guy
friend
We back and forth texted and he started to say he…
Liked me… Led me on. He had a girlfriend…
Then he said come over my GF's on vacation
So I did a huge mistake
He hooked up with me….
I thought he liked me…
1 week later I get a text to get out of your school.
His girlfriend and 15 others came including
Himself…
The girl and 2 others just said look around nobody
likes you
In front of my new school (50) people…

A guy then yelled just punch her already
So she did… and threw me to the ground a punched
me several times
The kids filmed it. I was all alone and left on the
ground.
I felt like a joke in this world…I thought nobody
deserves this :/
I was alone… I lied and said it was my fault and my
idea
I didn't want him getting hurt, I thought he really
liked me
But he just wanted the sex… Someone yelled punch
her already
Teachers ran over but I just went and laid in a ditch
and my Dad found me
I wanted to die so bad… when he brought me home I
drank bleach…
It killed me inside and I thought I was gonna actually
die
An ambulance came and brought me to the hospital
and flushed me
After I got home all I saw was on facebook – She
deserved it. Did you wash the mud out of your hair –
I hope she's dead.
nobody cared … I moved away to another city to my
mom's
another school… I didn't want to press charges
because I wanted to move on
6 months have gone by… people are posting pics of
bleach, Clorox and ditches
tagging me… I was doing a lot better too … They
said …
She should try a different bleach.
I hope she dies this time and isn't so stupid.

They said I hope she sees this and kills herself.
Why do I get this? I messed up but why follow me.
I left your guys city… I'm constantly crying now…
Every day I think why am I still here?
My anxiety is horrible now. I never went out this
summer.
All from my past… lives never get better .. I cant got
to school
meet or be with people … constantly cutting. I'm
really depressed.
I'm on anti-depressants now and counseling and a
month ago this summer
I overdosed. In hospital for 2 days
I'm stuck … what's left of me now … nothing stops
I have nobody I need someone :(
My name is Amanda Todd.

If you or someone you know is in such a place, and you are a Facebook user who comes across a friend's post that is alarming or causes great concern - like Amanda's video - you can help them! Read FB's *New Suicide Prevention Safety Feature* at https://goo.gl/jrA2ZI, then watch https://vimeo.com/160565004. *From Reporting to Supporting: Using Facebook to Support Someone in Suicidal Crisis.*

Talk to an adult you can trust, too. If you are the adult, connect with the minor in your life in a way that enables them to come to you in times of crisis, and they need your emotional support. Try to reassure them that they have done the right thing by telling someone, and acknowledge that it must have been difficult for them to deal with. Reiterate that no-one has a right to do that to them and that you are going to help them find a solution or elevate it to someone who can. It is essential to advise the minor being bullied not to take revenge in any way or respond angrily to any of the messages or emails. This is not so easy, but responding with anger, is probably what the bully would expect and by refusing to do this, the bully is thrown off guard and might discontinue their actions. If there is a need to respond, it should be done in an assertive manner, and with support. It depends on the situation, but given a couple of common scenarios with a more appropriate reaction would be to not respond and ignore the bullying behavior is often effective if the message is private. If the message is public then take action to report, delete, or block the post or message. Also, the victim could ask a friend to come to their assistance and help by standing up with them constructively and assertively. If the situation is beyond control, then encourage that minor to keep any evidence of the bullying activity and this information will be used to share with teachers, counselors, or the school principal. Bullying and hate crimes are against the law. If the matter is not resolved from there, take the situation to the police. If teachers or administrative members at your school refuse to take action, file a complaint or charge against the school for negligence in cases of criminal bullying. It is their job to ensure the safety of your child while they are at school. This could make the difference between ending the bullying and saving a minor's life as a result of BullyCide.

It is a legal obligation for a school district to protect its students from bullying and to address the issue when it occurs.[20] There are state laws that require schools to address these issues and every issue must be investigated and properly reported. It also must be reported to the federal U.S. government for Civil Rights Data Collection School Climate and Safety reports. Bullying in any form is a direct interference with the educational process and there are legal obligations if it is not dealt with properly. Overall, bullying affects school attendance and school performance. There are many programs that schools can adopt for anti-bullying which can have a positive effect, where students feel comfortable and safe to report incidents of bullying within their school. A learning environment should be both physically and emotionally safe for students, as well as teachers to be a more useful place for learning.

In Summary, the best things to do when you are cyberbullied:

- Do **NOT** reply to the bully!
- Tell Someone, such as an adult
- Parent
- Teacher
- Counselor
- Coach
- Religious Leader
- Hotline / SMS / TEXTING
- Principal

- Use Online Blocking Features

- Adjust Security Settings

- Threaten Action

- Report them to a site, school, parents, or law enforcement

There are national, local, and civil laws against cyberbullying, and the severity of those laws will depend on the filing location. Every State in the USA has a law in place. For example, in the State of Indiana, it is a Level 6 felony to stalk another person or make a threat intended to cause the victim reasonable fear of sexual battery, serious bodily injury, or death. (Ind. Code Title § 35-45-10-5).

Indiana law defines "stalking" as a knowing or intentional course of conduct involving repeated or continuous harassment that would cause a reasonable person to feel terrorized, frightened, intimidated, or threatened, and that does cause the victim to feel that way. (Ind. Code Title § 35-45-10-1).

A person convicted of a Level 6 felony of stalking faces imprisonment of 6 months to 2.5

years, a fine of up to USD 10,000 or both. (Ind. Code Title § 35-20-2-7). A person convicted of a Class B misdemeanor harassment by obscene message faces incarceration of 180 days, a fine of up to USD 1,000 or both. (Ind. Code Title § 35-50-3-3).

The aim of this pocket guide is neither to give legal advice, nor to provide counsel for any related matters, but if you would like to reference existing cases or codes by jurisdictions and keywords, visit *Find Law for Legal Representatives* at https://caselaw.findlaw.com/.

HOW TO PREVENT CYBERBULLYING

Some steps can be taken to minimize cyberbullying from happening in the future. Firstly, it is important to express to the minor the need for careful management of their personal information they share online and with whom. The majority of online networking and email sites allow the user to set their level of privacy and security. This ability to block, delete, and filter within networks and email is something all users should be made aware of when using online technology. It is also worth mentioning the obvious that BEFORE you 'Post' or 'Send' remember to think about whether you would want your family, friends, principal, coach, or future university or employer to see it? Also, if you hit the "Like" button in a cyberbully posting, this makes **<u>YOU</u>** a cyberbully too; *even without your words.*

Amanda Todd's tragedy sparked the awareness that social networking services have features that allow users to report and/or respond to cyberbullying in constructive ways. The TEEN Wellness chapter in this pocket guide provides additional information on how to respond to harassment and how to report cyberbullying material on social networking services and websites. Several signs can help indicate that a minor is a victim of bullying.

- Makes excuses not to attend school
- Has unexplained injuries, damaged or missing clothing or other belongings
- Avoids certain places or playing outside alone
- Stays isolated and withdrawn
- Low self-esteem
- Changes in eating habits
- Has trouble sleeping
- Has fewer friends
- Blames themselves for their problems
- Feels helpless
- Drastically alters behavior
- Talks about suicide
- In hindsight, parents & guardians should also

be aware that their child could be bullying others.

There are some signs to be aware of for minors who are actively bullying others such as:

- They are extremely competitive and must win and be the best at everything

- They do not accept responsibility for their actions

- Unable to control their anger

- Become frequently violent

- Manipulative and controlling of others and situations

- Blames others quickly

It is important to understand warning signs to help prevent children from becoming bullies or to not become a victim of a bully. Minors who are confident and have good self-esteem are less likely to fall prey to the attacks of a bully.

CHAPTER 4

IDENTITY THEFT

Unless you have been affected by it, you might never give the question much thought. Identity theft is when someone uses your personal or financial information to perform financial or legal transactions in your name without your knowledge. It is statistically shown that 1 in 11 children will be a victim of identity theft. If you become the victim of identity theft *(also discussed in the 'ID Theft Victims' chapter)*, chances are it will cause severe damage to your finances and your good name, especially if you do not find out about it immediately. Even if you do catch it quickly, you can spend months and thousands of dollars to repair the damage done to your credit rating. Worst-case scenario, you can even find yourself accused of a crime you did not commit because someone used your personal information to commit the crime in your name.

This is why it is so crucial that you secure your personal information in the best way possible.

Unfortunately, identity thieves are just waiting for you to make a mistake or get careless; there are many different ways thieves go about stealing personal information, e.g.

Steal Wallets / Backpacks – Identity thieves will steal your wallet, purse, or backpack to obtain a debit/credit card, driver license, bank deposit slip, or anything that contains your personal information.

Prevention tip: Try to keep important information to a minimum, keep it as separate as possible. If you must carry something, make sure that it cannot easily be taken. Over the shoulder, messenger-style bags are the best to carry in crowded places. Also, try to keep things in the front pockets of your pants rather than the back pockets.

Steal Mail – This is when mail is stolen directly from an unsecured mailbox *(which is a federal offense)* to steal someone's personal private information. This is serious because that might include bank or credit card statements or, worse yet, tax forms that include your Social Security number. Also, thieves will sometimes get your mail redirected by filling out a change of address request at the post office.

Prevention tip: A mailbox can be locked or secured from everyone except you and the mail carrier, as long as it meets USPS regulations. These regulations are noted at https://www.mailboss.com/guide-usps-mailbox-regulations/.

"Dumpster Diving" – Is a way that criminals will dig through your trash to find personal private information that might help them steal your identity.

Prevention tip: All trash that is discarded that contains names, addresses, or any other personal information should be shredded. If you do not have a shredder, just take a pair of scissors or tear the paper in places where the information is sensitive.

- Steal Registration or Insurance Card
- Rob your house
- Email Scams

Phishing – It was mentioned previously, but phishing is the act of tricking someone to click on a link. Once you click on the link, it will provide the criminal or fraudster with access to your personal private information.

Prevention tip: Before acting on an email link or attachment, investigate it thoroughly to make sure it is legitimate. If it appears to be from a company with whom you are familiar with, type in the URL yourself. Making a fraudulent email look legitimate is what identity thieves do.

Skimming - When skimming from an ATM, thieves attach card readers (called skimmers) over the legitimate terminal card reader to collect data from every card swiped. Other tactics are to place a fake PIN pad over the real one to capture victims' PINs (personal identification numbers) as they enter them, or installing tiny cameras. Skimming can occur anytime someone with a digital card reader gains access to your credit or debit cards. It can be done easily when the card is surrendered, such as in restaurants where it is common practice for a waiter to take the card to another area to swipe it. Once thieves have collected the stolen information, they can log into an ATM and steal money from the harvested accounts, or clone the credit cards to sell or for personal use.

Using chip-enabled cards whenever possible will cut down on the threat. Make sure you're signed up for fraud alerts for your credit and debit cards and that the pertinent apps for them are enabled. To thwart cameras and prying eyes on the low-tech side of things, do what you can to obscure any direct view when you enter your PIN (Personal Identification Number).

These <u>thieves</u> will use your information to:

- Buy Merchandise

- Open New Accounts *(creating fake social media accounts)*

- Get a Smartphone

- Open a Bank Account

- Take out a Loan.

Several signs could indicate that you have had your identity stolen; these consist of but are not limited to:

- Unexplained Charges

- Inaccuracies on your Credit Report

- Collection Calls from past due accounts

- Denied credit for no reason

- Receiving Credit Cards that you did not order

- Not receiving any bills.

There are oftentimes circumstances where there are security breaches. A security breach happens when data or records containing personal information, such as social security numbers, credit card or bank account numbers, or driver license numbers are lost, stolen, or accessed improperly. This kind of information can be used by criminals to commit identity theft, too. Being notified that your information was part of a security breach does not necessarily mean you will become a victim of identity theft. However, you are at greater risk and need to take steps to protect yourself.

Step 1: Check accounts that were affected: If the security breach involving credit cards, debit cards, or specific accounts, check your statements for those accounts immediately. If you see any activity that you did not authorize, immediately contact the bank or company that services the account to report the fraud. You should also request a new credit or debit card with a different number and change any PINs or passwords for the account.

Step 2: Sign Up for Free Services: There are some businesses or government agencies that offer security breach victims a free service such as credit monitoring. While most offers are genuine, do not provide private information without verifying that the credit monitoring service is legitimate.

Step 3: Notify the Credit Bureaus: You can request a fraud alert from one of the credit bureaus. This tells banks and other creditors to take extra steps to verify your identity before issuing credit in your name. A fraud alert is free and will last 90 days unless you request an extended seven-year fraud alert and provide a police report. You will also get a free copy of your credit report, which you should review carefully. Detailed contact information can be found in the 'References & Resources for TEEN health' chapter of this pocket guide.[23]

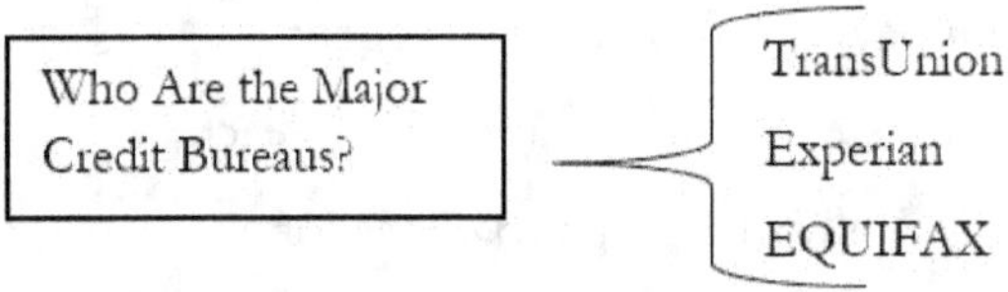

Step 4: Consider a Security Freeze: A security freeze stops access to new credit in your name. Placing a security freeze prohibits credit reporting agencies from releasing any information about you to new creditors without your approval, making it difficult for an identity thief to use your information to open an account or obtain credit.

Step 5: Monitor your Credit: Continue to review your credit reports every few months. Your private information that was released in the security breach might not be used right away. To get your free annual report from each of the big (3) mentioned above - TransUnion, Experian, Equifax - at www.AnnualCreditReport.com. The website is operated by those credit bureaus and authorized by federal law. You can access each of your reports once every 12 months for free. So, if you order your TransUnion credit report on

September 20, you cannot get another free copy until September 21 of the following year. After that, you can pay to receive more frequent copies, which usually cost around USD15 each, or you can typically order all 3 together for a discounted price. You might find this helpful if you have requested changes to your credit reports or filed a dispute and want to confirm that the information has been updated.

Step 6: Notify Law Enforcement: Most law enforcement will not issue you a police report until your private information is used by an ID thief. If you have any suspicion that your information is being used by a thief, contact local law enforcement immediately.

CHILDREN'S SECURITY FREEZES

There is a tool to help minors under the age of 16 from becoming victims of identity theft, called a Security Freeze or a Credit Freeze.[2] Parents of children under the age of 16 can set up a security freeze for their children. Guardians or those who have written legal authority to protect incapacitated adults can also get security freezes for those protected consumers.

Having a security freeze in place for children and other protected consumers prevents anyone from taking out credit in the minor or protected consumer's name. One of the most damaging forms of identity theft happens when criminals open a new account in someone else's name, so having a security freeze is an important tool to help keep a child or protected consumer's name and Social Security number from being used to open lines of credit. This control began 21 September 2018, and you can freeze and unfreeze your credit file for free. To set up a Protected Consumer security freeze, you will be asked to provide proof of identification for the protected consumer and the parent or guardian, including:

- Social Security Number or Social Security Card;

- A certified or official copy of a birth certificate, or;

- A copy of a driver's license or other government-issued identification;

You will be asked to provide proof of authority to act on behalf of the child or protected consumer. This includes:

- A court order;

- A value power of attorney;

- A document issued by a government entity showing proof of parentage, such as a birth certificate, or;

- Documentation from a county department certifying that the protected consumer is in a foster care setting;

Credit bureaus must comply with online or telephonic requests for a security freeze within one business day of receiving them. The credit bureaus must comply with requests made by mail within three business days of receiving them.

There are differences between a "Freeze" and "Locks", although they work similarly. A "Lock" could have a monthly fee, whereas a "Freeze' is a guarantee by federal law. As of 21 September 2018, an additional law covers 'year-long fraud alerts'. A fraud alert tells businesses that check your credit that they should verify with you before opening a new account. Previously, you could do this, but it would only last for 90 days. Now, when you place a fraud alert, it will last for one year. Fraud alerts will remain free and identity theft victims can still get an extended fraud alert for 7 years.

If you are enlisted in the military, then you have a slightly different advantage where you will still have access to active duty alerts, which let you place a fraud alert for one year, renewable for the time you are deployed. The active-duty alert also gives you an added benefit: the credit reporting agencies will take your name off their marketing lists for pre-screened credit card offers for two years (unless you ask them to add you back on).

You can place a fraud alert or active duty alert by visiting any of the above nationwide credit reporting agencies.

ID THEFT VICTIMS

If you have been the victim of identity theft, you can take steps to reclaim your good name and restore your credit. To make certain that you do not become responsible for any debts incurred in your name by an identity thief, you must prove that you did not create the debt.

Taking action quickly is important. Create a personalized recovery plan at identitytheft.gov that walks you through each step of the process. You can use the site to print pre-filled letters and forms to send to credit bureaus, businesses, and debt collectors, track your progress of recovering from ID theft, and update your plan. As you begin the task of reclaiming your good name, there are a few things to keep in mind:

You should track how much time and money you spend to clear up the problem, in case you can get restitution from the thief.

Keep Record and maintain good notes (especially keep your originals) on all of your dealing with creditors and law enforcement. Write down dates, contact names, addresses, phone numbers, and other details. Request a written confirmation of actions that have been taking regarding your case.

It is also a good idea to try to file your police report where the crime occurred because the case is more likely to be investigated there. If you can, file it where you live or where the suspected thief lives. If you file a police report, it will help to trigger helpful protection under both federal and state laws in the USA, such as an extended fraud alert and a free security freeze, which prevents access to new credit in your name as previously discussed.

Through identitytheft.gov, you put together information to create an ID Theft Affidavit, which - coupled with your police report - creates an "Identity Theft Report" that you then use to contact creditors to try to restore your credit.

Note that as a Victim of Tax ID Theft you can file an IRS Form 14039 if you are a US citizen.

Further, you should examine any medical records, if you suspect that someone has used your name to see a doctor, get medication, or file a health insurance claim. Patients who discover that they have been victims of Medical ID Theft must make efforts to get the information in their files corrected. You have a right to access your personal medical records per HIPAA (Health Insurance Portability & Accountability Act of 1996). A patient can submit a medical records request, and their personal medical records must be provided within 30 days to the patient. This law applies to any form of access to your medical records, whether they be electronic medical records or paper medical files. It depends on your location, but records request from your doctor for accessing a personal health record can be a written or verbal request, so check with your personal health practitioner to see what their procedure is.

If you have a driver's license, then you need to notify the DMV (Department of Motor Vehicles), if you suspect that someone else has a state-issued driver license in your name.

If someone is using your social security number for employment purposes, contact the federal and state authorities. You should alert the Social Security Administration in the USA at 1-800-269-027.

PROTECT YOUR ID ONLINE

Your online identity is created each time you use a social network, send a text, or make a post online. This means that your online identity is associated with YOU (either real or imposture) – the associated user – through authentication, when you 'register' or 'log-on'. Your online identity is your internet identity, internet persona, or social identity that an internet user establishes in online communities and websites.

It is even possible that your online identity could be different from your real-world identity from the way your friends, parents, and teachers think of you. Part of the fun of online life is trying on different personas. You can alter the way you act and present yourself to others (avatars), and you can learn more about things that interest you. The same as in your real life, you can take steps to help you stay in control of your image. But when you are online you do not always get a chance to explain your tone or what you mean. Thinking before you post and being responsible can help you avoid leaving an online identity trail you come to regret. There are some things to consider that will help you to safeguard your online identity and reputation. Protect pins and passwords for your devices, e-mails, personal information.

SAFEGUARD YOUR DEVICE

- Keep virus protection software up to date

- Install a firewall

- Use strong passwords/passphrases to protect your devices

- Do NOT store financial account information on your devices

- Do NOT store Personal Identification Numbers (PINs) or account numbers on a device that is accessible from the Web

- Use Wi-Fi wisely

- 'Wipe' your device clean before you sell, donate, or recycle it.

PROTECT YOUR EMAIL

Delete emails that contain confidential information[25]

It is often asked whether deleted e-mails are really 'deleted'. The answer is: "it all depends", namely on what email program or service you use, and it is not so easy to tell for certain. In the majority of the email programs and web interfaces, deleting an email message does not delete it. Instead, the message is simply moved to the "trash" or "deleted items" folder. It depends on your program or service, but most online services automatically delete emails from the "trash" after a certain amount of time (usually around 30 days), or you can empty the bin manually as well. That gives you a month to change your mind and recover anything you did not mean to delete. However, it cannot be presumed, whether or not that program or service is actually deleting these messages!

There is also the impact of your 'service provider' backing up your system when it comes to retrieving emails. An online email service could get a legal request to retrieve your emails from their backups. This means, even if you have completely deleted an email, that service could still recover it from the backups they took while the email was in your account.

Emails can also be retrieved from the copy in the sender's Sent mail folder, and the copy that the recipient(s) receive(s). Regardless of who you are – sender or recipient – it is always possible that the email message might be recoverable from the other party to the communication.

- Do NOT respond to emails - especially from overseas - asking for your help to transfer money, even when the circumstances described appear to be of an emergency nature.

- Beware of emails that ask you to confirm your personal information or account number, even when the email appears to come from a legitimate business, bank, or charity

you know. This is called phishing.
Forward these emails to
spam@uce.gov. This is used only for
SCAM type spam, not spam in
general.[24]

- Check with your internet service
  provider about security features, such
  as how to block spam.

- If you suspect hacking or email
  tampering, report it to your local law
  enforcement.

- Be careful about clicking on links
  provided in an email, and never such
  links sent by someone you do not
  know.

PROTECT YOUR PERSONAL INFORMATION

Never provide your social security number or financial account numbers online unless it is through a valid, secure website. Secure websites often have a lock icon in the lower right-hand corner. A secure website address will change from HTTP to HTTP**S** (Hypertext Transfer Protocol Secure), which is an internet communication protocol that protects the integrity and confidentiality of data between your device and the website that is being used. HTTP**S** protects your connection by using built-in certificates to show that that particular website has been authenticated. This means that the website has been tested for encryption, data integrity, and authentication, and the certificate was issued by a certificate authority, which takes steps to verify that the web address belongs to that organization, thus protecting its customers from man-in-the-middle attacks.

- Be careful about providing any personal information online, but keep in mind that some government sites and credit bureaus require this information. Read privacy policies and ask how your personal information will be used.

- Do NOT post personal financial information on social networking sites or in chat rooms or social media boards.

- Choose an alias as a username and use an alternate email address for online shopping, internet auctions, and other online transactions.

PROTECT YOUR PINs & PASSWORDS

If someone logs on to a site and pretends to be you, they can trash your identity. Pick passwords that no one will guess and change them often. Never share them with anyone other than your parents or a trusted adult. Not even your best friend, boyfriend, or girlfriend should know your private passwords!

- Do NOT share your PINs or passwords with other people

- Do NOT carry PINs or passwords in your wallet or purse

- Do NOT use the same PINs or passwords for more than one account
    - If any one of your passwords gets compromised, that puts all the accounts where you have also used it at risk. Every second around the world there is an increasing number of sophisticated hackers who try to break into devices, and they <u>succeed</u>!

To protect yourself you should, ideally, be using a different password for every account. If you only have a handful of accounts, then you can probably just remember them. However, most of us have so many accounts that it would be very difficult to remember them all.

- Avoid using the information for your PIN or password that could be easily guessed based on the information you post on social networking sites.

- Avoid using easily available information for your PIN or password such as your mother's maiden name, your birth date, SSN, phone number, or a series of consecutive numbers (for example 1234).

WHERE CAN I SAVE/STORE MY PASSWORDS WHEN I HAVE SO MANY?

The notion of simultaneously being 'secure' and 'convenient' are usually not in sync with each other. When you make something more secure, you are also likely to make it less convenient. It's unfortunate, but it is a modest cost in comparison to the consequences of being 'hacked' and your accounts stolen and sabotaged. It's important to measure the risks against the benefits, and think about your worst-case scenarios, and then make a decision that is most reasonable given your circumstances.

Today, there ARE cloud-based password-storage services or "password manager" which have become very popular recently. These services or applications typically store your passwords in a secure, encrypted database that might be located on your device, but is also stored online (in the cloud) and can be synchronized between your devices. As long as you remember your master password, you can access all of your passwords from any device for all your accounts. You need to understand that while a 'password manager' is convenient and sophisticated, you also remember that you are storing your data online – and that – by definition is LESS SECURE than the data that you store only on devices in your possession. If you use a "password manager", then you trust that the service that you are using is storing your data securely, allowing you availability and access as and when you need it, your stored information will not be hacked, they will not lose or sell your data to someone else (like the government), keep your account open, not go out of business, or put your data at risk, even if it is encrypted. It is not clear on how these services are backing-up their data, which in turn reduces the ability for you to protect your data/identity! If you want to use a "password manager" or "iCloud" storage, then know that your information is _in the clouds_, too – literally!:)

Ideally, there are some reasonable methods to secure this kind of information, such as:

Puzzles: Invent your method, secret code, or abbreviations to mask your passwords. For example, if you create a convention that "A" stands for "Aaron" and "B" stands for "Bill", then writing "A123" or "7B!" on your password list would not give a thief any useful information to break into your accounts, as long as you do not write down what "A" and "B" stand for.

Passwords can be stored using a password-management software that stores encrypted information only on your device and not in the cloud. You can choose a strong master password for the database. If you need passwords when you're on the road, either print them out (be extremely careful with that printout, and shred it when you get back) or use a program that offers a companion application for your smartphone or tablet that can sync over your local network, not via the iCloud. Use a password-management software that runs on your local network ONLY (your network at your home, not the school, Starbucks, McDonald's, etc.), and avoid the iCloud. Here are some password-management software sites where you can run both Windows & Macintosh, such as:

- http://www.splashid.com - SplashID
- http://www.agilebits.com - 1Password
- http://www.jointlogic.com - B-Folders
- http://www.PasswordWallet.com - PasswordWallet
- http://www.iliumsoft.com - eWallet
- http://keepass.info - KeePass *(Windows only)*

On your computer, you can create an encrypted folder using encryption software and a strong password.[26] You can move your document labeled "Passwords" (do not call the actual filename: Password) and other sensitive files into it, lock the file when not in use, and then securely delete ("shred") the original, unprotected document. There are several good tools to use for creating general-purpose encrypted folders on your computer such as:

- http://veracrypt.codeplex.com
- http://winzip.com

For MacOS, the .dmg file format is another secure storage option that is already built-in. If you want to learn more, you can just google, 'create encrypted .dmg'.

If you have created a paper password chart, then lock it in a desk or filing cabinet when you are not using it, which is away from family, cleaning staff, visitors, and others. If you do not have a key lock, consider using a combination lock to eliminate having to store & copy keys.

To securely delete/shred files on your computer, you can use certain tools such as:

Windows: http://eraser.heidi.ie

MacOS: Use 'Delete Immediately', which will overwrite your drive's free space.

CHAPTER 5

Wi-Fi / FREE Wi-Fi
#WirelessFidelity

Wi-Fi is an abbreviated term for "Wireless Fidelity", the standard developed by IEEE that enables devices to connect with wireless networks. It is a form of wireless technology that is very widely spread and can get you connected almost anywhere, such as home libraries, schools, airports, work, hotels, and even restaurants. The word 'Fidelity' in its most simplistic terms means <u>loyalty</u> or <u>faithfulness</u>. One of the main advantages of Wi-Fi is that it is integrated into many different information technology devices such as PCs, smartphones, tablets, printers.

What is a Hotspot? The term Hotspot is used to define an area where Wi-Fi access is available. This can either be through a closed wireless network at home or in public places such as restaurants or airports. A wireless adapter should be included, to access Hotspots. If you are using an advanced laptop model, it will probably include a built-in wireless transmitter already. If it does not, you can purchase a wireless adapter that will plug into the PCI slot or USB port. Once installed, your system should automatically detect the Wi-Fi Hotspots and request a connection. If the Hotspot is not detected, then the software can be used to help assist in connecting to the Hotspot.

** Risks associated with using Public Wi-Fi **

The biggest threat when using Public Wi-Fi is the entire exposure of your data, activity, and identity. The majority of people who use public Wi-Fi - falsely - think that their information is protected. The majority of people logging onto public Wi-Fi are checking their e-mails, using social media, accessing financial or bank information. Any of those details could be stolen if the Wi-Fi connection is insecure.

How can I tell when I am using a secured website? When you are browsing on a website and the URL address begins with http://, meaning it is using **H**yper**t**ext **T**ransfer **P**rotocol, but it does not have an added security layer. When you switch to purchasing financial or sensitive personal information that URL should change, to begin with, http**s**:// and the image of a 'lock' should appear, too. For those of you who are visual learners, the browser will look like this:

"FREE" Wi-Fi Safety

There are many hidden dangers to using Public Wi-Fi, just to name a few are:

- Do NOT use anything that requires the use of a Login

- Do NOT log into Social Media

- Do NOT engage in any credit card transactions

- Do NOT do any online banking

- Do NOT open your e-mails, or where you have to enter a username or passcode.

What can I safely do on Public Wi-Fi?

- Watch a video or a film on Netflix

- Read the news

- Check the weather

- Check the Traffic Conditions

- If you have your GPS / locator on your phone, your applications will be able to track where you are, especially if you are sharing your location!

- Check airline flights/train times.

What are these "Cookies" that I hear about all the time? Why does it matter?

Cookies are a small text file that a Web server downloads to and stores on your device. If you are looking for 'Converse tennis shoes' on the internet and you have your GPS locator turned on; you will begin to receive publicity or advertisements about 'Converse tennis shoes' on sale in the area that you are in. Cookies hold' the data of the user, such as their name and preferences, and use that to solicit goods or services. Cookies are used for several purposes:

- Customize web pages

- Store usernames and passwords, so that you do not have to log in each time

- Tracks which web pages or ads that you have visited

- Keeps track of your items in an online shopping cart, so that you can go back later and purchase those items if you wanted to.

You should be aware that websites SELL cookie data, or use third-party cookies to record clickstream data from any Web page or link. The companies who buy this information, then turn around and use it to create more targeted advertising. For example, have you ever noticed that the same banner advertisements seem to follow your browser as you click through various internet pages? Why do the boys have ads about sports cars and motorcycles or motocross, whereas the girls could have make-up, clothes, or hairstyle advertisements? As mentioned at the beginning of this pocket guide, Google knows you well. Some sites make assumptions about you and use these assumptions to place you in an advertising program based on your online activities and try to calculate what interests you. Surprisingly, the information companies collect about you from a variety of sources to make these assumptions. For the moment, cookies are driven by what the user is feeding it. Directly behind this is a more advanced method that is underway called cross-device tracking called SilverPush. This is where advertisers are using subsonic signals, where the sounds are too low or too high for people to hear to force internet access devices to communicate with each other. For example, SilverPush technology can also insert subsonic audio into television commercials that can be "heard" by your device without you even knowing the connection exists. This method uses device proximity in real work to discover more information about you, rather than relying on your internet activities. As mentioned in the Acknowledgements, if you want to not be tracked with your internet activity with cookies, then you will use one of the internet search engines that emphasize protecting searcher's privacy.

It is not the objective of this pocket guide to expand on too much detail about the diagnostics or the technical aspects as to whether our technical devices are 'spying' or 'listening' to their customers, but there are some basics to be aware of. The virtual assistants that are common today are Siri, Alexa, Google, etc. If you give a command like "Hey Siri" or "Okay Google" then there are certain privacy implications to consider. Ideally, your iPhone listens to you when you give 'consent' for them to do so, but keep in mind that all technology companies operate in different ways and you should be concerned about your privacy. It's not certain if certain applications and technology are really only listening to a certain command, and at this time it is a controversial topic between technology giants and lawmakers. However, you can opt to stop these applications from listening to you, by opening 'Settings', and then tap off the toggles for that application to listen and also toggle off for when your phone is locked (when you're not using it). There could still be applications that can bypass these settings, and perhaps you could tape over your microphones, as well as covering webcams. It is just as important to make you aware of smart televisions with voice activation and voice recognition, where it is also controversial that there is a possibility that conversations could be heard. You can take measures to control your privacy by turning off the Smart Interactivity on your television.

1. Press the menu button on the remote control
2. Select settings
3. Highlight Smart Interactivity
4. Press the right arrow to change the setting to "Off".

PUBLIC CHARGING STATIONS

#ATTENTION

Your smartphone can easily be hacked if you plug it in to charge via a USB in public places like airports, coffee shops, amusement parks, hospitals, or while on public transport. There are three different ways to charge a mobile phone battery.

1. Power cord plugged directly into a socket
2. The USB-based charger that draws power from another device's USB port.
3. Placing your smartphone/smartwatch on an inductive charging pad.

**If you start to PANIC because you really cannot wait to begin charging at an electrical socket, then turn your phone completely OFF before plugging it into the charging station.

CHAPTER 6

FAKE / FALSE DOCUMENTS
(Driver License, Passport, etc.)

Falsifying documents is a felony; a conviction can mean jail, fines, and probation depending on the offense, i.e. to buy alcohol, cigarettes, or a firearm; Class 1 Misdemeanor for possession, distribution, or usage vs. Class 6 Felony for firearms. Fraudulent documents facilitate terrorism, smuggling, drug & human trafficking, immigration violations, and many other crimes. Some of the most significant crimes and terrorist attacks in recent times, including 9/11, were made possible through fake IDs. These and other fraudulent documents enable criminals to escape detection, conceal their true identities, and pass through borders undetected.

Possession of a 'Fake ID' is serious. Criminal charges have long-lasting effects on your future. It affects your ability to concentrate on both work and school and can cost you time and money in attorney fees and possibly fines. Though everyone seems to do it, you can decide for yourself. Avoid the possible consequences, only use your valid identification or driver license.

Note: Facial Recognition by the BMV (Bureau of Motor Vehicles) helps secure Driver License authenticity. An L-1 identity solution is used to cleanse databases of duplicate photos. If there are multiple photos for a single driver's license because of license renewals, then each license holder is matched.

In the USA, there are several security features on a DL to detect if it is false or not, such as:

1. A vertical DL will indicate that the driver is under 21 years of age;
2. The dates when the driver will turn 18 & 21are highlighted on a DL;
3. The Gold State symbol in the upper left indicates that it is an Operator License;
4. There is digital enhanced texturing on the face of the DL;
5. A Gold Star symbol in the upper right will indicate a 'SecureID Credential';
6. A watermark is visible under black light on the face of the DL.
7.

PROTECT YOURSELF
(Teen To-Do LisT)

There are global Cyber Intelligence Professionals that are working non-stop to fight cybercrime and initiate civil proceedings all over the world. These professionals subpoena *(request to provide documents or to appear in court)* phone companies and service providers to obtain metadata, IP addresses, and other identifying information to try and fight injustice and educate the public about the proper usage of the internet for YOUR safety. Metadata is any information that helps describe some aspect of the data being reviewed. For example, metadata is similar to putting information in different buckets, such as documents, images, videos, etc.

There are many billions of people using the internet than there are fraud fighters, so we need your help to take measures to protect yourself. You must keep conscious of the fact that your information could always be used or spied upon just because you crossed paths with someone who is being investigated. If you have an internet presence, there is and always will be data collected about you, not to mention facial recognition applications that have surfaced in recent years as well. When you are in Paris or the UK, you are captured on video cameras roughly 70 times per day!

It is important to keep in mind that anybody can use the information you have left behind to uncover your secrets to hurt or judge you in ways that might cost you a future job, a relationship, your pride, or even your reputation. You should know - and expect - that EVERYONE is looking at you! This includes your school, employer, a stalker, an identity thief, your future husband/wife, the FBI, coaches, the local police, etc. Once you've interacted on the internet, you've given ANYONE access to your information. So, it's important you know and understand what you're doing and use privacy settings as much as you can to control your internet identity, as previously explained. As a Certified Fraud Examiner, I have performed hundreds of audits. As a teenager, you are not at this level – but before each investigation or interview, I research my subjects the best way as I can simply by searching online on who they are. I know who they are and a lot about them BEFORE I have even met them. People will do the same thing to YOU, one day. Whether you apply for a job or at university or want to join a team; someone will try to "Google" you.

THE WORLD IS WATCHING YOU!

The internet is simultaneously a privilege and a curse. Some things can be done to help minimize the risk of being a victim. There are a few easy steps that you can adopt to help protect yourself. I encourage you to use these preventative - and even detective tasks - on yourself to make your virtual and actual environment a more secure place. Here is a 'To-Do' list for yourself, not in any particular priority:

✓ Perform a financial Self-Audit on yourself

✓ There are 3 credit reporting agencies such as Experian – TransUnion – Equifax. *You can find the contact information in the chapter on Teen Wellness.* Parents can FREEZE the accounts of their minors in the USA from consumer purchases.

✓ Use search engines to find YOURSELF online, by performing a <u>people</u> search. Find out what the internet is saying about you because there are only two ways that information can exist about you online. The first is social content that was created by yourself, and the second is the content created by third parties. To see how you appear online, conduct a personal audit – of YOURSELF. To get started, enter 'YOUR NAME' in one of the follower browsers:

- Google.com

- Bing.com

- Pipl.com

- Yatedo.com

- Spokeo.com

- Peekyou.com

- Foupas.com

- yoName.com

- NameChk.com

✓ Maximize your security settings on every electronic device used

✓ TURN OFF / SHUT DOWN your device(s), often

✓ Clear your browser(s) history regularly

- ✓ Create passwords not so obvious to those who know you *(no names, no birthdates, no anniversaries, etc.)*
- ✓ Stand up to cyberbullies!
- ✓ Shred your mail if not used, e.g. bank loan offers credit card offers, etc.
- ✓ Buy a cross-hatch shredder or cut with scissors every single piece of mail that has your name on it *(especially if you live in an apartment or share community trash units).* **Attention** If you are at a university/college, all companies want to give you a credit card because they know you will be making money soon. Do not just throw those away without shredding the offer first!
- ✓ Have an e-mail address that is **<u>not</u>** your full name. It is implicit that you will want an e-mail address if you are a student looking for work so that you can be identified by your name, but you do not have to use this for a majority of things. Quick Story: I went to an indoor trampoline park in the USA not too long ago. Upon my arrival at the counter to

pay, I was requested to sign a 'Waiver' and give my full name, birth date, and address. I saw all these people giving their personal, confidential information to this trampoline park just so that they could jump. I found this to be for commercial use only and DID NOT give this information as it is just being used for analytics to help them with their marketing. It is a marketing ploy relying on the term "Waiver", but believe me, if you broke your leg while jumping, they would be able to take this information then. Be careful with your personal information and know what people will be using it for. In this situation, I gave an e-mail address that did not contain my name, and I encourage you to do the same.

✓ What **<u>NOT</u>** *(sorry to constantly Italicize and Bold, but it is so important to stress these points)* to do while you are online:

✓ DO NOT put information out there that can haunt you later on.

✓ Jeopardize college scholarships & future job

applications

✓ Be aware of what others could write about you (future ex-friend) & upload photos that perhaps shows you in a 'less flattering light'.

✓ DO NOT put other people's personal contact information on inappropriate sites, i.e. X-rated sites, dating sites, etc.

✓ Serious consequences for both the person you are victimizing plus possible legal constraints against you.

✓ NEVER *(1000 times never!)* ever arrange to meet with someone you only know 'online'. If I was standing in front of you right now, you would say "I know that", but it is beyond my comprehension to truly understand how these crimes continue to happen. I suppose that it is a mixture composed of being naïve, vulnerable, trusting, hopeful, charmed, or even manipulated that continue to make these sorts of crimes proliferate. It is nice to receive attention, even have someone to talk to, but please be extra cautious in these situations. Attorney experts for Cybercrime say that nine of ten cases begin with "I met him online".

✓ NEVER give out your personal details such as your phone number, address, passwords, or photos.

✓ DO NOT accept or open e-mails, IM messages, file attachments, pictures, or texts from people who you do not know.

✓ Make it a rule for yourself, because you need to respect yourself, to NOT text / SMS and drive at the same time. If you researched this, you will find there are thousands of teenagers that are doing this; and you put yourself and others at such a risk. If you are in a very important conversation, you can just pull the car to the side and finish your conversation, or utilize a call hands-free on speakerphone.

CHAPTER 7

TEEN WELLNESS & OUTREACH
#CalltoAction

A healthy, well-balanced lifestyle for minors is our biggest hope. The teenage years can be especially tough, and since there is no comparable solution for every child, we have gathered a list of resources for your reference, if and whenever so needed. Emotional, physical, social, environmental, occupational, intellectual, and spiritual wellness is crucial for anyone to be able to work towards healthy wellness habits for life. Sometimes it takes reaching out and asking for help in order to overcome the obstacles that face us.

Many people feel as though there is no solution, and then they lose hope. You are **<u>NOT</u>** alone, so if you need some support and guidance, the most important thing is not to try and endure your struggle on your own.

As parents, the best thing we could do is to stay in contact with our 'minor' online and offline without making them feel like we are controlling their every move, as this does not go over so well. *For parents who want to know how to accomplish the 'control' factor is well explained by the Child Development Institute. They explain that nobody likes being 'controlled' and that we can only control situations, and that relationship factors are as important as rewards and punishments in how 'people' respond to control.*[27] By doing this, it will allow you to see their "virtual world' and it can help them feel more comfortable coming to you if they need any advice or support. It is important to let your minor know that you have a trust and an 'open door' approach with them to encourage them to talk with you openly about concerns that they might have, without fear of you judging them or quickly criticizing them. Let your minor speak to you, and try to listen to what message they are trying to 'openly' give to you. Even if it is something that you will not be able to fix, your support and guidance are necessary for helping them find an appropriate solution. I believe I saw this next point on LinkedIn, but it was talking about how most people only, "listen to respond, and not necessarily to understand". For the sake of your minor and the consideration of the time and emotions they spend on their online profiles, and how anything said about them online can have a profound impact (either positive or negative); it is important to listen and understand their concerns. They will often hesitate to reach out for advice because the first thing that a parent would do is to restrict their internet access or remove their social media accounts. Take your time to assess the situation and control your reaction in a way that will not prevent them to come to you with their problems or concerns.

REFERENCES & RESOURCES FOR TEEN HEALTH

USA & CANADA

EMERGENCY MEDICAL HELP
Dial 911

HELP Dial 211 or http://211.org
Nation-wide service available in all languages connecting over 14 million people to services every year, such as:
- *Supplemental Food & Nutrition programs*
- *Shelter and Housing options and utility assistance*
- *Emergency information and disaster relief*
- *Employment and Education opportunities*
- *Services for Veterans*
- *Health Care, Vaccination and Health epidemic information*
- *Addiction prevention and rehabilitation programs*
- *Re-entry help for ex-offenders*
- *Support groups for individuals with mental illnesses or special needs*
- *A safe, confidential path out of physical and/or emotional domestic abuse*

SUICIDE

Suicide Prevention Lifeline/+1 800 273 8255
www.suicidepreventionlifeline.org
24-hour, toll-free, confidential suicide prevention hotline available to anyone in suicidal crisis or emotional distress. Your call is routed to the nearest crisis center in the national network of more than 150 crisis centers.

The Trevor Project (LGBTQ)
+1 866 488 7386 https://pflag.org/hotlines
Lesbian, gay, bisexual, transgender, and questioning young people ages 13-24

LGBT National Youth Talkline
+1 800 246 7743
https://www.glbthotline.org/talkline.html
help@LGBThotline.org
The Lesbian, Gay, Bisexual, and Transgender (LGBT) Youth Talkline provides telephone, online private one-to-one chat, and email peer-support, as well as factual information and local resources for cities and towns across the USA.

Crisis Text Line
Text START to 741-741
https://www.crisistextline.org/
Crisis Text Line is free, 24/7 support for those in crisis. Text from anywhere in the USA to text with a trained Crisis Counselor.

CYBERBULLYING

Cyberbully Hotline   +1 800 829 0067 www.byberbullyhotline.com

TEEN LINE   +1 310 855 4673 & +1 800 852 8336

Sexually Exploited Photos   +1 800 843 5678

National Center for Missing & Exploited Children www.report.cybertip.org

The Cyber Civil Rights Initiative +1 844 878 CCRI www.endrevengeporn.org

Woman against Revenge Porn www.womenagainstrevengeporn.com

Without My Consent www.withoutmyconsent.org

C.A. Goldberg, PLLC www.cagoldberglaw.com

The Cyber Civil Right Legal Project www.cyberrightsproject.com

**Note: The New York Law School, home of the cyber-harassment Clinic, is part of the Tyler Clementi Institute for Safety, providing pro bono representation to victims of cyber harassment.

ACT –Adults & Children Together -Against Violence
ttp://actagainstviolence.apa.org/

BOSTON vs. BULLIES
http://www.bostonvsbullies.org/

Bullying.org
http://www.bullying.org/

Eyes on Bullying
http://www.eyesonbullying.org/

National Youth Violence Prevention Resource Center
http://www.safeyouth.org/scripts/topics/bullying.asp

No Bully
http://nobully.com/

PACER National Center for Bullying Prevention http://www.pacer.org/

PREVNet
http://www.prevnet.ca/

Stop Bullying Now!
http://www.stopbullying.gov/

Bullying Activity for Any Classroom
https://www.youtube.com/watch?v=-j6foVLceD8

IDENTITY THEFT

FTC
+1 877 438 4338
www.ftc.gov/idtheft www.identitytheft.gov

U.S. Department of Health
+1 800 368 1019
(Medical ID Theft) www.hhs.gov/ocr

On Guard Online
www.onguardonline.gov

Stop Fraud
www.stopfraud.gov

ID Theft
www.idtheft.gov

United States Postal Inspection Service
https://postalinspectors.uspis.gov

Social Security Administration
 www.ssa.gov

Federal Bureau of Investigation (FBI)
www.fbi.gov

NON-PROFIT RESOURCES FOR IDENTITY THEFT

Consumer Action
www.consumer-action.org

Identity Theft Research Center
www.idtheftcenter.org

National Fraud Information Center
www.fraud.org

Privacy Rights Clearing House
www.privacyrights.org

AARP (American Association of Retired Persons) www.aarp.org/money/scams-fraud
+1 877 908 3360

National Association of Attorney General
www.naag.org

Equifax Security:
FREEZE, P.O. Box 105788 Atlanta, GA 30348
+1 800 349 9960

Experian Security:
FREEZE, P.O. Box 9554 Allen, TX 75013
+1 800 397 3742

TransUnion:
TU Protected, Consumer Freeze, P.O. Box 380
Woodland, PA   +1 800 916 8800

ADDICTION

National Council on Alcoholism and Drug
Dependence   +1 800 622 2255

Drug-Free America runs a drug hotline for
PARENTS +1 855 DRUG FREE (378-4373)

The National Poison Control Center
(Overdose)   +1 800 222 1222

CANADIAN CENTER for CHILD PROTECTION / CENTRE CANADIEN de PROTECTION L'ENFANCE

https://protectchildren.ca/pdfs/ItisaBigDeal_en
..pdf

PARENTING TWEENS AND TEENS IN THE DIGITAL WORLD

https://protectchildren.ca/pdfs/C3P_Parentingi
ntheDigitalWorld_en.pdf

ÊTRE PARENT DE PRÉADOS OU D'ADOS À L'ÈRE NUMÉRIQUE

https://protectchildren.ca/pdfs/C3P_Parentingi
ntheDigitalWorld_fr.pdf

FRANCE & some UK

Suicide Écoute   +33 (0)1 45 39 40 00
https://www.suicide-ecoute.fr online ChatLine

S.O.S Help   +33 (0)1 46 21 46 46
www.befriends.org or
https://www.soshelpline.org/ *(daily 15:00-23:00)*

Terror/kidnapping hotline   197

Directory inquiries   12

SOS emergency housing for the homeless
115

Rape hotline   +33 (0)8 00 05 95 95

Racial discrimination helpline   114

Victims of violent crime hotline
+33 (0)8 10 09 86 09

Domestic violence helpline   3919

**SOS child abuse Service National d'Accueil
Téléphonique de l'Enfance en danger**
Call 119
http://www.soshelpline.org/gethelp.html

Any Problem big/small (UK)
www.childline.org.uk or +44 (0)800 1111
(<19 years of age)

The Mix Organization
www.themix.org.uk   +44 (0)808 808 4994
(13:00-23:00) (<25 years of age)

Police Nationale 17 or +33 (0)1 39 10 91 00 or
112 mobile

Youth Mental Health   116 123
jo@samaritans.org

Police Municipal   +33 (0)1 30 87 23 62

Fire brigade   18 or 112 mobile
SAMU & Emergency medical 15
Child Abuse   119
Missing children   116 000
Sexual Abuse   116 006
Drug info service   +33 (0)800 23 13 13
Aids info service   +33 (0)800 84 08 00
SOS friendship   +33 (0)1 42 96 26 26

SOS Victimes 78   +33 (0)1 41 83 42 08
https://francevictimes78.fr//

Youth Violence Listening +33 (0)808 807 700

Violence Conjugales   3919

**Le Centre d'information sur les droits des
femmes et des familles (CIDFF)/
Institute of Reproductive Health
(women victims of violence)**
+33 (0)1 39 10 85 35
Tobacco info service   3989

CYBERBULLYING / CYBERHARCELEURS

French Bullying Hotline
5 3020 or +33 (0)800 200 000
Mon-Fri 09:00-18:00

Family Lives Helpline (UK)
+44 (0)808 800 2222
Mon-Fri 09:00-18:00 Sat-Sun 10:00-15:00

ACAS helpline (UK)
https://www.bullyonline.org
+44 (0)300 123 1100

Haas Avocats
http://www.haas-avocats.com
Le projet de loi LOPPSI 2 a inséré dans son texte un article relatif au délit d'usurpation d'identité « numérique », pour lequel il est prévu une peine d'emprisonnement de 2 ans et de 20 000 EUR d'amende (article 2).

IDENTITY THEFT

Service-Public.fr
https://www.service-public.fr/particuliers/
vosdroits/F10774

Assitôt.fr
https://www.aussitot.fr/facebook/signaler-
compte-pirate-usurpation-identite-facebook.html

Condexatedenbay.com
https://www.condexatedenbay.com/comment-
savoir-si-quelqu-un-a-vole-mon-identite/

FCFrancoisCharron.com
https://www.francoischarron.com/vol-didentite-
et-faux-profil-facebook:-quoi-faire/-
/kTJbBzMgdv/

ADDICTION

SOS Help   +33 (0)1 46 21 46 46
www.soshelpline.org
(Mon-Sun 15:00-23:00)

Suicide Écoute   +33 (0)1 45 39 40 00
www.suicide.ecoute.free.fr

E.P.E. IdF, FII Sante Jeunes
www.filsantejeunes.com
+33 (0)800 235 236

Fédération S.O.S Amitié +33 (0)1 40 09 15 22
www.sos-amitie.com
+33 (0)1 46 21 46 46 in EN

LOST OR STOLEN CREDIT CARDS

American Express   +33 (0)1 47 77 72 00
Visa   +33 (0)8 92 70 57 05
Master Card   +33 (0)800 901 387
Citibank (collect call)   +1 605 335 2222

TREATMENT CENTERS

Treatment centers are programs that provide support to answer all questions about recovery in a wide range of subject areas. The different types of subject areas teens can struggle with are:

- Bullying

- Depression / Anxiety

- Video Games / internet / Device (Ab)Use / Electronics

- Self-Harm

- Mental Health

- ADHD (Attention Deficit Hyperactivity Disorder) / ADD (Attention Deficit Disorder)

- Sex / Abuse / Trauma

- Eating Disorders

- Tobacco / Marijuana

- Alcohol / Drugs / Substance Abuse

Treatment centers or treatment programs consist of dedicated people who are compassionate, professional, and well-educated who help find solutions and recovery for teenagers. The typical rehabilitation services and programs can include a range of options depending on your circumstances. A plan can be developed with or for a teen that is most suitable for them, which could consist of:

- Intervention
- Detox
- Psychiatric Evaluation
- Medication Management
- Individual Therapy
- Support Groups
- Academic Programs

The needs of every teenager are individual and specific. If all remedies have been exhausted and you are considering a treatment option that is best suited for your situation, focus your time and energy on a facility that will meet your exact needs. If you have reached this point, it is evident that you feel helpless and will go to all ends to find the most appropriate and strategic choice possible to find a solution to the problem that you are faced with. It is most likely that you might not always be able to decide for yourself and 'tough-love' by a parent is being forced, or in certain cases, the choice could be legally mandated, if the minor has been arrested or convicted of a crime. If outpatient treatment is ordered, you would need to work with the court-appointed counselor or officer to work out the details of the treatment. This is often called a diversion program. It also depends on the type of issues that the minor is facing, but certain therapy might only be for the individual, family, or even a group. The type of therapy is circumstantial between all the variables that are impacting a teenager. Treatment programs are offered either on an outpatient basis, allowing a teenager to live at home, or in a more structured residential (in-patient) program. Treatment programs can also be gender-specific. Residential programs provide full-time treatment within a secure, residential setting. This type of program is most appropriate for teens whose behavior is dangerous, whose outpatient treatment has proven unsuccessful, or who risk harm from someone at home. Outpatient programs are those that provide treatment during the day while the teenager continues to live at home at night. These options are often the best place to start if you agree and fully believe that:

✓ The teen poses no risk to himself/herself or others at home.

✓ Family dynamics will not interfere with the teen's ability to overcome their problems.

Here are some well-known treatment centers (search for your particular location).

USA & CANADA

All Conditions for Treatment, Rehabilitation, or Recovery

1. https://www.treatment-centers.net/directory.html
2. http://www.childrenshospital.org/conditions-and-treatments
3. https://www.rehabs.com/top-rated-treatment-centers/

Addiction to Drugs – National Rehabilitation Directory

1. https://addictionresource.com/drug-rehab/teen/
2. https://www.rehabs.com/teen/
3. https://local.rehabreviews.com/
4. http://rehabcenters.com
5. https://www.alltreatment.com
6. https://teenrehab.interventionamerica.org/
7. http://drugrehabcenters.us.com

Video Games / Internet / Computer Use / Electronics Addiction

1. https://www.sovteens.com/treatment-programs/teen-behavioral-health/internet-addiction/
2. http://familybootcamp.org/teen-internet-addiction
3. https://www.gamequitters.com
4. https://www.legrandchemin.qc.ca/parents/
5. https://starguideswilderness.com/
6. https://paradigmmalibu.com/teen-internet-addiction-treatment/
7. https://thecanyonmalibu.com/blog/teens-and-internet-addiction/
8. https://bluefirepulsar.com/young-adult-internet-addiction/
9. https://www.crchealth.com/troubled-teenagers/internet-addiction-teenagers/
10. https://www.midwoodaddictiontreatment.com/

11. http://www.techaddiction.ca/children-addicted-to-video-games.html
12. https://www.easrehab.com/
13. https://www.smartrecovery.org/teens/
14. https://www.marylandaddictionrecovery.com/
15. https://www.banyanpalmsprings.com/
16. https://americanaddictioncenters.org/treatment-centers/resolutions
17. https://landmarkrecovery.com/
18. https://maplemountainrecovery.com/

Sex / Abuse / Trauma / Mental Health

1. https://www.centerforvictims.org/services/victim-services/
2. http://rehabcenters.com/sexual-abuse
3. https://www.psychologytoday.com/us/treatment-rehab/sexual-abuse/california
4. http://www.satchawaii.com/
5. http://www.therapyassociates.net/
6. https://drugabuse.com/sexual-abuse-treatment/
7. https://www.therenewcenter.com/
8. https://ubhdenton.com/treatment-services/adolescents/
9. https://thecenteratpiw.com/our-programs/
10. https://ridgeviewinstitute.com/
11. https://universitybehavioral.com/programs-services/children-and-adolescents/adolescent-dialectical-behavior-therapy/
12. https://www.therefuge-ahealingplace.com/ptsd-treatment/

13. https://www.sheppardpratt.org/care-finder/the-trauma-disorders-program/
14. https://www.life-healing.com/search/sex
15. https://www.recoveryranch.com/
16. https://riveroakshospital.com/programs/adolescent-psychiatric-program/

Eating Disorders

1. https://www.eatingdisorderhope.com/treatment-for-eating-disorders
2. https://luxuryrehabs.com/condition/eating-disorders/
3. https://www.edreferral.com/edcenters
4. https://thetreatmentspecialist.com/mental-health/eating-disorders/
5. https://www.alsana.com
6. https://centerforchange.com/eating-disorders
7. https://www.timberlineknolls.com/eating-disorder/
8. https://eatingdisorder.care/
9. https://www.nationaleatingdisorders.org/treatment
10. https://goop.com/wellness/health/good-programs-for-eating-disorder-treatment-and-recovery/
11. https://www.rosewoodranch.com/
12. https://www.montenido.com/
13. https://renfrewcenter.com/
14. https://www.theeatingdisordercenter.com/
15. https://www.psychologytoday.com/us/treatment-rehab/eating-disorders/ga/atlanta

16. https://riveroakshospital.com/programs/eating-disorders/
17. https://www.sierratucson.com/eating-disorders/

Cyber-Bullying

1. https://solsticertc.com/about-us/
2. https://americanaddictioncenters.org/trauma-stressor-related-disorders/effects-being-bullied-harassed
3. https://www.therecoveryvillage.com/drug-addiction/related-topics/bullying/
4. https://www.ridgefieldrecovery.com/drugs/related/bullying-and-drug-abuse/
5. https://www.amethystrecovery.org/bullying-and-substance-abuse/
6. https://www.villagebh.com/disorders/bullying/
7. https://perspectivesoftroy.com/bullying-treatment-options/
8. https://www.goodtherapy.org/learn-about-therapy/issues/bullying/bullying-support
9. https://www.sevenhillsbi.com/disorders/ptsd/bullying/
10. https://pro.psychcentral.com/cyber-bullying-recognizing-and-treating-victim-and-aggressor/
11. https://centerforanxietydisorders.com/school-bullying/
12. https://www.mindpathcare.com/mental-health-treatment/bullying/
13. https://www.montenido.com
14. https://toledocenter.com/

15. https://www.mcleanhospital.org/treatment/klarman
16. https://www.sovhealth.com/treatment-programs/eating-disorders/
17. https://www.alohacares.com

CANADA REHABILITATION CENTER(S)

1. https://www.drugrehab.ca/ontario-residential-drug-rehab.html

FRANCE

All Conditions for Treatment, Rehabilitation, or Recovery Addiction to Drugs

1. https://www.drogues-info-service.fr
2. http://www.ifac-addictions.fr
3. https://www.addictaide.fr
4. https://annuaire.lefigaro.fr/annuaire/region/ile-de-france/centre-addictologie
5. https://sos-addictions.org/
6. https://www.desintoxicationdrogue.fr/

Video Games / internet / Computer Use / Electronics Addiction

1. http://www.addictauvergne.fr/echelle-addiction/internet-addiction-iat/

Cyber-Bullying

1. https://www.jurifiable.com/conseil-juridique/droit-penal/harcelement-sur-internet
2. https://www.service-public.fr/particuliers/vosdroits/F32239

CHAPTER 8

DELETE YOURSELF FROM THE INTERNET *(if you want)*

The internet is a global network of billions of electronic devices with unlimited access to information, communication, work (alternative to 9-5 workdays), school, relationships, marketing, sexuality, self-expression, and - fortunately - help. The internet is one of private consumption without the need for naming yourself. There could arrive a moment where you want to RETURN to the time when you did not have as much exposure on the internet. By the privacy and anonymity factor of cyberspace, the internet can work with you or against you, but YOU have to be the one to take control or have the control of your personal information. If you have a negative image online, or just want to lay low for a while a decision can be made to 'delete; yourself from the internet. How you could entirely remove yourself from the internet is circumstantial and depends on your exposure and information that you are wanting to delete. Also, if you shared and downloaded a photo or message, it is hard to have control over that and if you follow these steps your social media presence will fade, and only the copy that you shared with someone will be stored wherever they copied it to.

In any case, follow these simple instructions to try and minimize &/or delete the information about you as much as possible.

SEARCH YOURSELF

The first step is to search for yourself on Google. Begin by searching just your name. See what google shows on both the web, images, and videos. Google Search might not be for a people search engine, but it seems to give good information as a starting point. You can search for people through names with specific keywords like location, job, interests, etc. It is also possible to do a reverse phone number search and if you have a photo of the person, you can do a reverse image search to find the person you want. Another special feature on Google is its ability to offer various tools like filters for time, country, and an advanced search page, where you can narrow down your search easily. On a more advanced note, if you wanted to see your visibility with actual 'People' searches, then the most popular sites being used are as follows:

- Pipl
- BeenVerified
- Whitepages

- Spokeo
- PeekYou
- Intelius
- Facebook
- InstantCheckmate
- LinkedIn
- Mylife

DELETE YOUR SOCIAL MEDIA ACCOUNTS

It is uncertain what your activity level is on social media, but if you are serious about deleting yourself from the internet; the most important step is to delete your social media accounts. Profiles on sites like Facebook, Twitter, Instagram, and YouTube often have lots of information on you. The key is to *delete,* rather than *deactivate.*

Facebook

Facebook provides options for both deactivation and deletion of a user account. Deactivation keeps your account ready for a quick return to the site. Deletion instigates the process of wiping your stored data and prevents Facebook from accessing your information, as long as you do not log in for the two-week quick reactivation period. To skip over the deactivation process and go right to delete is a bit trickier than you might think. Web searches will likely bring you to the deactivation page.

Instead, https://www.facebook.com/login.ph

p?next=https%3A%2F%2Fwww.facebook.com %2Fhelp%2Fdelete_account takes you straight to deletion. Hit **Delete My Account** and check your email for a confirmation. To more fully wipe your presence before deletion, you might want to consider disconnecting Facebook from other applications and wiping your activity history. You also have the option of downloading your Facebook data to keep for your own records before deletion.

Twitter

Similar to Facebook, you can begin your process by archiving your Twitter account. Then, you can start to follow the steps toward deletion. (In this instance, you will want to follow the path toward "deactivation.") Click your photo icon and proceed to *Settings and privacy*. Then, scroll to the very bottom of the page, where you will see a link to **deactivate your account.** Click and follow the prompts to finish the deletion process.

Snapchat

The main thing to note here is you cannot delete your Snapchat account from your mobile app. You must go to a computer for Snapchat.com. Once logged in, go to *Delete Your Account* page in *Accounts*. You need to enter your login information, then choose *Delete My Account*.

Instagram

Instagram also has an option for temporary disabling or deleting. If you want to say goodbye for good, you will be looking for permanent deletion. You cannot delete your account from the Instagram app, you have to do it from a computer. On a browser, go to the Instagram 'Delete Account page'. You will be asked to let the company know your reason for leaving, and to enter a password. Then you can opt for account deletion.

CONTACT WEBMASTERS

If you run across information that has been published about you online – such as in a news article or blog – you will need to contact the webmaster in charge of the website. In most cases, they will need to physically delete the content. You do not have a whole lot of control.

REMOVE YOURSELF FROM DATA COLLECTION SITES

A multitude of companies on the internet collect your information to sell it to advertisers and other interested parties. Some major ones include Spokeo, PeopleFinder, and Whitepages.com. While it is possible to access each of these sites one by one and have your information removed, it is a pretty cumbersome process. Every site has its own unique policy. Some require you to fax them physical paperwork, while others make you get on the phone. *"Anyway, an easier way to do it is to use a service like DeleteMe at Abine.com,"* Eric Franklin writes for CNET. *"For about USD 130 for a one-year membership, the service will jump through all those monotonous hoops for you. It'll even check back every few months to make sure your name has not been re-added to these sites."*[28]

CHAPTER 9

CAREER DEVELOPMENT
www.acfe-france.fr or www.acfe.com

What am I going to do when I graduate from High School? There are just so many choices, it is so difficult to choose; it is an uneasy feeling to possibly choose the wrong 'major' or 'subject' that I will not be good at or even like. This is a normal and universal feeling every student has in every single country around the world. We all think about our future and have dreams of doing something fun and interesting, while at the same time making a lot of money doing it. There could be some students that have a goal 'just to graduate' or some to 'graduate early', or even some to not even finish school and perhaps return later. No matter what the scenario is, life will almost insist that you choose something. In the end, it will be YOU who has to live your life and undergo the circumstances of whichever road you choose. We can be encouraged, persuaded, or even pushed by our parents, teachers, professor, or peers; the road might not be a 'perfectly straight' one, but the idea is to keep going forward with something and you will eventually slip into your place. Have confidence in yourself and know that each one of us has something to give and receive.

If you have a special interest in the field of 'Business', in particular, if you would like to be a Fraud Fighter, here are some topics I share with you to point you in the right direction.

<u>No. 1 - Take the right Courses</u>

- ➢ Criminal Law
- ➢ Finance/Accounting
- ➢ Crime Scene Investigation
- ➢ Computer Fraud
- ➢ Internal/External Auditing
- ➢ Psychology/Interviewing
- ➢ Computer Systems
- ➢ Database Management
- ➢ Information Security
- ➢ Economics
- ➢ Accounting/Computer Forensics
- ➢ Statistics

No. 2 – Look for Internships:

➢ Networking plays an integral role

➢ Well-targeted resume & cover letter

➢ Solid Interview skills

➢ Academic Credits

Websites to help search for jobs:

- Indeed.com

- Internships.com

- Careershift.com

- Idealist.org

- Experience.com

- Internmatch.com

- Usajobs.gov

- Mediabistro.com

- Internabroadusa.com

- Internships-usa.com

- Wayup.com

No. 3 – Communication Skills
(*recommendations*)

➢ Learn a 2nd/3rd language

➢ Speak with passion and purpose

- ➢ Develop personality
- ➢ Do not be afraid to fail
- ➢ Do not be afraid of hard work
- ➢ Express your voice
- ➢ Display creativity
- ➢ Have a healthy sense of humor
- ➢ Make Connections
- ➢ Speak plainly
- ➢ Have stories to tell

<u>No. 4 – Significant Credentials *(obtain Certifications)*</u>

- ➢ CFE Certified Fraud Examiner
- ➢ MBA Master of Business Administration
- ➢ CIA Certified Internal Auditor
- ➢ CPA Certified Public Accountant
- ➢ CISA Certified Information Systems Auditor
- ➢ CCEP-I Certified Compliance & Ethics Professional – International
- ➢ CAMS Certified Anti-Money Laundering Specialist

CONCLUSION

Fortunately, not all people become victims of cybercrimes, but everyone is potentially at risk. We have become heavily dependent on the internet for many reasons, which has given rise to countless opportunities in various fields such as banking, entertainment, gaming, business, and education to name but a few. As you have learned, cybercrimes vary greatly, they do not always occur 'behind the device', but they are executed in some technological way. A hacker's identity ranges from 12 to 67 years of age. People who commit cybercrimes could be living three continents away from their victims - or right next door!

Given the information in this pocket guide, you are strongly encouraged to think before you post. Standing up for yourself and your beliefs is important, but there are also courteous ways to share your opinion. You never know who is watching or reading, so do not post dangerous or wicked opinions. Do not swear or curse, do not insult other people, do not spread hatred, and do not bully other people. Your behavior is likely to circle back around to you (Karma); as the Golden Rule states: "Do unto others as you would have them do to you", or in its most simplistic form: "Treat others how you would like to be treated".

It is crucial to keep your personal life as private as you can. Unfortunately, the wrong person can stumble upon your birthdate or address and misuse that information for criminal purposes. Sharing too much of your personal information can put you and your family at risk. You also run the risk of allowing followers and strangers to know too much about you. If you have personal accounts on Facebook and Twitter, a blog, or a personal web page, keep those things private. Use embedded security features; never accept a friend or follow requests from someone that you do not know. There is a theory that, if you have many friends on Facebook, it means you are very popular. It is much better not to look so desperate, using smart cyber practices to keep you safe and, in turn, look good to the people who do follow you online.

The material in this guide merely scratches the

surface of the in-depth information available to share with you. In time, it is anticipated that there will be a stronger collaboration between governmental organizations, internet service providers, and the education system to fight against bullying, school violence (both physical & psychological), and cybercrimes.[6]

The purpose of my effort is to inform children, teenagers, families (especially naïve elders), friends, teachers, parents, and school board members about the tools and tips needed to build, protect and enhance their internet identity. It does not have to be a discouraging experience on the internet. There are many ways that you can constructively participate and benefit from the opportunities that the internet has to offer. It is my fervent hope that you will remember some of the facts you have gained from this pocket guide and begin to build, grow, and maintain an appropriate internet image of yourself.

CYBER VOCABULARY

Online safety & internet security pose many dangers, requiring extreme caution to navigate through all the various vocabulary terms. The list below considers most of the major words or phrases relating to the internet the technology that we are using today; derived from the Cybersmile Foundation website, a non-profit organization for anti-cyberbullying & digital wellbeing.[1]

419 Scam type of advance fee fraud asking to help transfer money out of another country; originated in West Africa, 419 is a section of Nigerian legal code that covers the crime.

802.11 standard for wireless networks.

A

Access Control Controlling who has access to what information.

ActiveX Controls can enhance your browsing experience by allowing animation or help with tasks such as installing security updates at Microsoft Update. If you do not trust the website & publisher, click 'Don't run' when prompted.

Administrator user with sufficient access rights to allow them to manage the access rights of other users & carry out other high-level device management tasks.

Advance Fee Fraud any fraud that tricks victims into paying money upfront in the

false hope of receiving
something significant later.

Adware form of spyware that displays unwanted advertisements on a device.

AIM AOL's instant messaging system.

Android operating system used by many device manufacturers. The world's most prolific operating system for smartphones.

Antispyware Software specifically designed for detection & prevention of spyware. Often bundled in an Internet security package.

Antivirus Software is specifically designed for the detection & prevention of known viruses. Often bundled in an Internet security package.

ATM Automated Teller Machine: a cash machine often referred to as a 'hole in the wall'.

Attachment files, such as programs or documents that are attached to an email.

Authentication process for verifying that someone or something is who or what it claims to be. In private & public device networks (including the Internet), authentication is generally done with passwords.

B

Back Door loophole in a device's security systems that allows a hacker to gain access. Often deliberately built-in by developers for illicit purposes.

Backup copying data to ensure its availability in the case of device failure or loss.

Bandwidth speed at which a network can transmit data – typically used to describe the speed of Internet connections.

Biometric using bodily attributes, e.g. fingerprints & irises, as a means of authentication.

BIOS Password BIOS software is built into a device, first software that runs when powered up. It can be password protected, thereby stopping a device from starting up.

Bit basic binary unit of data, representing 0 or 1.

Bluetooth type of short-range wireless connection between devices like smartphones, headsets, computers, tablets.

Boot To start-up or reset a device.

Boot Password is needed before a device starts up or any operating system can be loaded.

Botnet collection of otherwise unrelated devices that have been infected by a virus, which are under the central control of criminals or hackers. Abbreviation for Robot Network.

Browser program that lets users read & navigate pages on the Internet, such as Microsoft *Internet Explorer*, Mozilla *Firefox*, Google *Chrome,* or Apple *Safari.*

Buffer region of memory in which data is temporarily held before it is transferred between two locations or devices.

Buffer Overflow when more information is added to a buffer than it was designed to hold. An attacker could exploit this vulnerability to take over a system.

Bug an error or flaw in a device program.

Byte unit or measure of device memory, usually consisting of eight binary digits (bits) processed together; usually enough to store a single letter or digit.

C

Certificate encrypted file containing user or server identification information, which is used to verify a website owner's identity & to help establish a security-enhanced link.

Chargeback process of reversing a transaction & returning payment to a customer – typically when goods have not been received or are faulty.

Chat Room online discussion group where you can chat (by typing) with other users in real-time.

Client application or system that accesses a service made available by a server – generally refers to a device on a network.

Cloud see Cloud Computing

Cloud Computing provision of storage & computing capacity to end-users via the Internet. Commonly used for backing up data & hosting applications.

Cookie small file asking permission to be stored on your device enabling web applications to personalize your experience by gathering & remembering your preferences.

Cracking finding a password or PIN by trying many combinations of characters, typically with specialized programs like L0phtCrack .

Critical Update software update that fixes a security flaw.

D

Data Protection Act 1998 sets out a legal basis for handling, processing, protecting personal data in the UK.

Decryption process of converting encrypted data back into its original, readable form.

Desktop Firewall software designed to prevent unauthorized network access to a device.

Digital Signature used to identify & authenticate the sender & integrity of message data. It can be bundled with a message or transmitted separately.

Discoverable status of a Bluetooth device set up to broadcast to other Bluetooth devices.

Distributed Denial Of Service Attack (DDOS) deliberate overloading of service by criminals to make it unavailable to legitimate users, e.g. by arranging millions of simultaneous visits to a website – normally from a Botnet.

Domain Name website address, alternatively known as a URL.

Domain Name Server (DNS) converts recognizable domain names, e.g. microsoft.com, into their unique IP address, e.g. 207.46.245.222.

Download obtain content from the Internet, as an email attachment or from a remote link, to your own device.

Doxware (Leakware) form of Ransomware in which the attacker threatens to publicize sensitive data obtained from the victim's hard drive unless a ransom is paid.

Dumpster Diving method of social engineering in which criminals raid rubbish bins to gather personal information from discarded letters, invoices, bank statements, etc.

E

Easter Egg unexpected 'feature' built into a device program by its author. It can be added for fun or with malicious intent.

Eavesdropping listening into voice or data traffic without the knowledge or consent of the sender or recipient.

Elevation Of Privilege when a user (particularly a malicious user) gains more access rights than they should normally have.

Email Attachment files, such as documents or photographs, attached to an email.

Email Filter software that scans incoming email for spam or viruses, or outgoing

email for viruses, and filters it
accordingly.

Encrypted see Encryption

Encryption process of converting data into
ciphertext (a type of code) to prevent it
from being read by an unauthorized
party.

Escrow trusted third-party service that holds
money, software, or other assets pending
completion of a transaction.

Executable File an .exe or .dmg (MacOS)
file used to install & run on devices.

F

Face ID biometric type of authentication
utilizing a user's face scan to identify
them, particularly on smartphones &
tablets as an alternative to passwords.

File-Sharing making files available over a
network to other users, typically music
or video files.

Fingerprint Recognition biometric type of
authentication utilizing fingerprints;
increasingly on devices as an
alternative to passwords.

Firewall hardware/software devised to
prevent unauthorized access to
devices/networks.

Freeloading where unauthorized users gain
access to your wireless network
connection.

FTP (File Transfer Protocol) method of
transmitting data files over networks,
normally between businesses.

Full Backup where all the chosen files are backed up, regardless of whether they have changed since the last backup.

G

Gateway Firewall that operates at the point where a private local area network connects to the public Internet.

Gigabyte 1000 megabytes.

Grooming process by which someone develops a relationship with someone else for illegal or immoral intent. Often used to describe how pedophiles develop relationships with unsuspecting children.

H

Hacker person who breaches device security for malicious reasons or personal gain.

Hard Disk fixed magnetic disk drive or solid-state used to store data on devices.

Hard Drive see Hard Disk

Hoax Email An email that makes a false claim with criminal intentions, for example, a virus warning. These emails might carry a real virus and are designed to make the virus spread rapidly.

Honey Pot security feature built into a network, designed to lure hackers into meaningless locations to avoid harm to genuine, crucial data.

Hotspot publicly accessible wireless Internet connection.

HTML (Hypertext Markup Language) device code that is used to form the basis for building web pages.

I

iCloud Apple's secure cloud storage &
backup product.

Identity Theft The crime of impersonating
someone – by using their private
information – for financial gain.

IETF Internet Engineering Task Force: the
body that defines standards underlying
the Internet.

**IMEI (International Mobile Equipment
Identification)** unique serial number
built into smartphones & tablets. To
determine a device's IMEI, dial *#06#
on the device.

Incremental Backup where only files that
have been changed or added since the
last backup are stored, making it faster
than a Full Backup.

Information Commissioner (UK) The
U.K. Information Commissioner's
Office (ICO) is the independent public
body set up to uphold information rights
in the public interest, responsible for
upholding the Data Protection Act 1998
& Freedom of Information Act 2000.

Information Security discipline of
protecting devices & data from misuse.

Instant Messaging Chat conversations
between two or more people by typing
on devices. Systems include BlackBerry
Messenger, Facebook Chat, Windows
Live Messenger, AIM Phoenix, Yahoo!

Intrusion Testing Legally hacking into a
device or website with the consent of the

owner, to reveal vulnerabilities, thereby finding opportunities for improving its security.

iOS Apple operating system used on its iPhone & iPad devices (see also **MacOS**).

ISP (Internet Service Provider) company that provides access to the Internet.

IP Address (Internet Protocol address) unique address used to identify a device on the Internet.

IPSec (IP Security) provides security for the transmission of sensitive information over unprotected networks such as the Internet. IPSec acts at the network layer, protecting & authenticating IP packets between participating IPSec devices.

IT Security see Information Security

J

Java One of today's most popular & widely used programming languages. Originally developed by Sun Microsystems (now Oracle).

JavaScript programming language derived from Java to make web pages more interactive.

K

Key Logger see Keystroke Logger

Keystroke Logger virus or physical device that logs keystrokes in order to capture private information, passwords or credit card information.

Kilobyte 1000 bytes.

L

Laundering see Money Laundering

Linux An open-source, freely-available operating system.

LAN (Local Area Network) for communication between devices - wired or wireless.

Log File that lists actions that have occurred on a device.

M

MacOS Apple's operating system used for its computers (see also **iOS**).

Macro type of program used to eliminate need to repeat steps of common tasks over & over, e.g. adding/removing rows & columns, protecting / unprotecting worksheets.

Macro Virus uses the macro capabilities of common applications such as spreadsheets & word processors to implement virus-like behavior.

Malware Software used or created by hackers to disrupt a device's operations, gather sensitive information or gain access to private systems. Short for 'Malicious Software'.

Megabyte 1000 kilobytes.

Memory Stick removable memory device normally connected to a device via USB.

Money Laundering process to conceal the source of money obtained illegally, by carrying out financial transactions or operating fake businesses to camouflage the illegal source.

Money Mule Someone who is recruited by a fraudster to transfer money illegally gained in one country to another country, usually where the fraudster lives. The term comes from an analogy with drug mules.

MP3 technology used to store sound files, typically for music or podcasts.

MP3 Player device that plays MP3 music files.

MSN Messenger see Instant Messaging

N

Network number of interconnected devices, together with the connecting infrastructure.

Non-Repudiation ability to prove that a specific individual has carried out an activity on a device or online, so that it cannot later be denied.

O

Online Backup method in which data is transmitted over the Internet for storage, often referred to as 'Cloud' backup.

Open Source term to generally describe software developed collaboratively, often by volunteers on a non-commercial basis.

Operating System software that enables your device to function.

Owned When a device has been taken over by hackers.

P

Padlock symbol in a web browser indicating an encrypted (SSL) connection is being

used to communicate with a site that has
a valid certificate. Normally
accompanied by 'https' at the beginning
of the address line.

Pairing when two Bluetooth-enabled
devices are linked to communicate with
each other.

Patch software update, often related to
fixing 'bugs', thereby improving security.

**PDF (Portable Document
Format)** method of saving a document
so that it can be opened & viewed on
devices using different operating
systems.

Peer-To-Peer network typically used to
share music/video files & applications
between individuals over the Internet.

Penetration Testing see Intrusion Testing

Pharming exploit in which criminals disrupt
the normal functioning of DNS
software, which translates Internet
domain names into addresses. The user
enters a correct address but is redirected
to a fake website.

Phishing attempt at identity theft in which
criminals lead users to a counterfeit
website in the hope that they will
disclose private information such as
usernames &/or passwords.

PIN Personal Identification Number

Ping a simple program that communicates
with another device over a network to
see if it is responsive.

Piracy illegal duplication/use of material covered by intellectual property laws, copyright.

Pop-Up small window that appears over a web page, usually to advertise.

Port physical or virtual connection in a device enabling applications to communicate with pre-determined external devices.

Premium Rate telephone number, typically prefixed by 09, which is very expensive when dialed. Often related to scams.

Privileged User Access see Privileges

Privileges access rights to devices or data – normally varying between users according to what they are/are not entitled to see & do, i.e. read, write, modify, delete.

Profile list of personal details revealed by users of social networking, gaming, dating & other websites. Profiles are normally configured to be either public or private.

Proxy Server that manages Internet traffic to & from a local area network and can provide other functions, such as Internet access control.

Q

QR Code designed to be scanned by a device's camera contains a link to a website belonging to the code's originator. Like a barcode, not readable by the human eye.

R

Ransomware form of malicious software (or malware) that, once it has taken over your device & encrypting your data, threatens you with harm, thereby denying access to your data. The attacker demands a ransom from the victim, promising - not always truthfully - to restore access to the data upon payment. Users are shown instructions on how to pay a fee to get the decryption key. Costs can range from a few hundred USD to thousands, typically payable to cybercriminals in Bitcoin.

Recordable DVD that is capable of storing data when used in a DVD recorder.

Removable Media storage devices that can be physically removed from a device, such as CDs, DVDs, USB sticks & portable hard drives.

Rootkit set of tools used by hackers to get control of a device.

Router device that routes network or Internet traffic. Typically found in-home or small office environments within a Wi-Fi device (wireless hub).

S

SamSam form of Ransomware that often attacks device systems. Developed privately & updated frequently, to avoid antivirus detection & other endpoint defenses.

Script Kiddies hackers whose illicit activity is for notoriety rather than criminal intent.

Security Exploit piece of software or sequence of commands that takes advantage of a software bug, glitch, or vulnerability to cause problems, often with criminal intent.

Server device that provides files or services to other devices over a network or the Internet.

Skimming act of counterfeiting bank cards with a device to capture account information embedded on the card's magnetic strip.

Smart Card form of user authentication that relies on a credit card-sized card with an embedded chip.

Smartphone A mobile phone built on a mobile computing platform, with more advanced computing ability & connectivity than a standard mobile phone.

Smishing practice of attempting to obtain personal or financial information via SMS to commit fraud or identity theft.

Social Engineering use of deceit offline to gain access to secure systems or personal information, for example, by impersonating a technical support agent.

Spam unsolicited commercial e-mail; also known as junk e-mail.

Spoofing when unauthorized persons send messages (typically emails) that appear to come from a genuine sender by using either a genuine or a very similar address.

Spyware malware that secretly monitors a user's activity or scans for private information.

SSD solid-state drive that uses integrated circuit assemblies to store data persistently, typically using flash memory like USB keys; supplanting traditional Hard Drives.

SSID wireless network name which enables users and Wi-Fi-enabled devices to identify one wireless network from another. Acronym for <u>S</u>ervice <u>S</u>et <u>ID</u>entifier.

SSL (Secure Socket Layer) an encryption system that secures Internet communications.

Sync to link devices - typically computers, smartphones & tablets - to ensure they contain the same data such as contacts, emails, music files, etc. Short for synchronizing.

T

Tablet ultra-portable, touchscreen device which shares much of the functionality and also the operating system of smartphones, but generally with more computing power.

TCP/IP Transmission Control Protocol/Internet Protocol, the conventions used by devices to communicate over the Internet.

Terabyte 1000 gigabytes.

Token physical object, such as a smart card, used to authenticate users.

Traffic transmission of information over a network or the Internet.

Trojan software posing as an authentic application, which conceals an item of malware. The term comes from Trojan Horse in Greek mythology.

Two Factor Authentication method of obtaining additional evidence of identity compared to simply using passwords, such as a one-time code transmitted by SMS.

U

URL Uniform Resource Locator a.k.a. as web address

USB (Universal Serial Bus) means of physically connecting devices & peripherals such as external storage, keyboards, MP3 players, etc..

Usenet Internet-based public bulletin board system that allows users to post messages to different newsgroups.

User Account gives individuals access to files & programs on a device, often controlled by the login.

Username code name that, with a password, unlocks a user account.

V

Virtual Private Network see VPN

Virus file written with the sole intention of harming and/or for criminal activity.

Virus Signature virus 'fingerprint' which contains the characteristics of a virus or type of virus. Internet security software uses a database of signatures to detect (known) viruses.

Vishing practice of attempting to obtain personal or financial information via a voice call to commit fraud or identity theft.

VoIP Voice over IP technology transmitting phone-like voice conversations via the Internet.

VPN (Virtual Private Network) method of creating a secure 'tunnel' between two points over the Internet. Normally used only for business-to-business communications.

Vulnerability any product flaw, administrative process or act, or physical exposure that makes a device susceptible to attack by a malicious user.

W

Webmail an email system that uses a web browser to read & send emails, rather than a standalone email program such as Microsoft *Outlook* or Apple *Mail.*

WEP (Wired Equivalent Privacy) data encryption type to prevent eavesdropping & access to a wireless network by malicious users. Defined by 802.11 standards.

Wi-Fi see Wireless Network

Wireless Hotspot publicly accessible wireless Internet connection.

Wireless Hub see Router

Wireless Router see Router

Wireless Network local area network using radio signals instead of wire to transmit data.

Worm type of virus that can spread itself across networks without human intervention.

WPA (Wi-Fi Protected Access) data encryption type preventing eavesdropping & access to wireless networks by malicious users. Defined by 802.11 standards. It provides stronger security than WEP.

WPA2 (Wi-Fi Protected Access 2) data encryption type preventing eavesdropping & access to a wireless network by malicious users. Defined by 802.11 standards. It provides stronger security than WPA or WEP.

REFERENCES

1. Madison Web Solutions. Language Glossary.
    https://www.cybersmile.org/internet-
    terminology

2. Federal Trade Commission. Identity Theft.
    https://www.consumer.ftc.gov/blog/2018/
    09/free-credit-freezes-are-here

3. Expatica. French Emergency Numbers &
    Support Helplines.
    https://www.expatica.com/fr/about/gov-
    law-admin/emergency-numbers-in-france-
    and-support-helplines-101100/

4. Légifrance Non-Harcèlement Le ministère
    de l'éducation Nationale et de la Jeunesse
    https://www.nonauharcelement.education.g
    ouv.fr/ressources/

5. RFI. *France Unveils Bullying Hotline for Students
    to Clamp Down on Harassment*
    http://www.rfi.fr/en/general/20151029-
    France-unveils-bullying-hotline-students-
    clamp-down-harassment

6. Ministère de l'Éducation Nationale et de la
    Jeunesse
    https://www.education.gouv.fr/pid33441/n
    ous-
    contacter.html#Prevention_des_violences_e
    n_milieu_scolaire

7. http://www.europarl.europa.eu/RegData/et
    udes/STUD/2016/571367/IPOL_STU(201
    6)571367_EN.pdf

8. Ben-Joseph, Elana Pearl, MD. *"Protecting
    Your Online Identity and Reputation."*
    TEENS Health 8 April 2018

https://kidshealth.org/en/teens/online-id.html

9.   Game Quitters. Video Game Addiction Support.
     https://gamequitters.com/respawn/

10. Kagan, Julia. *"Contactless Payment"*. Investopedia 21 June 2019
     https://www.investopedia.com/terms/c/contactless-payment.asp

11. Sweney, Mark. *"More than 80% of Children lie about their age to use sites like Facebook"* The Guardian - International Edition 26 June 2013
     https://www.theguardian.com/media/2013/jul/26/children-lie-age-facebook-asa

12. Dax the Duck. *"Protect your privacy in 2020 in 5 simple steps"*. DuckDuckGo Blog. 16 December 2019
     https://spreadprivacy.com/tag/device-privacy-tips/

13. Moore, Trent. *"What Happens to Your Body When You Play Video Games for Hours."* Grunge 19 October 2019
     https://www.grunge.com/26711/happens-play-video-games-long

14. Entertainment Software Rating Board. 5 April 2019. Ratings Guide.
     https://www.esrb.org/

15. Audio English. Org. 2019. Dictionary entry Overview.
     https://www.audioenglish.org/dictionary/corrupted.htm

16. Adaware Keep on Connecting. 2004. *"How to Detect Malware Infection on Your Computer"*

https://www.adaware.com/faq/how-to-detect-malware-infection

17. Manshoory Law Group – A Professional Corporation. 21 November 2017 *"The Consequences for Impersonating Someone Else, Including Police"* https://manshoorylaw.com/blog/the-consequences-for-impersonating-someone-else-including-police/

18. Haze, Meko. 25 December 2019. *"What is Swatting and How Can I Protect Myself from Being a Victim"* https://discussglobal.com/what-is-swatting-protect-myself-victim/

19. Huffingtonpost.com, CNN.com, Vice.com. Unknown. Fat Shaming. https://www.vice.com/en_us/topic/fat-shaming

20. Harper, Amelia. 2 October 2018 *"How are School Districts Legally Responsible for Bullying"* https://www.educationdive.com/news/how-are-school-districts-legally-responsible-for-bullying/538619/

21. Vancouver Film School/CC-BY 2.0. Unknown. https://www.reference.com/world-view/appearance-important-f1b85f73df4bb89c

22. Huffingtonpost.com, CNN.com, Vice.com. Unknown. *"Fat Shaming and Body Shaming"* http://www.bullyingstatistics.org/content/fat-shaming-and-body-shaming.html

23. The Balance 25 February 2020. *"What are the*

3 Major Credit Reporting Agencies"
https://www.thebalance.com/who-are-the-three-major-credit-bureaus-960416
24. Privacy Rights Clearinghouse. 2004. Spam.
https://privacyrights.org/about
25. Ask Leo! by Leo Notenboom. Unknown.
"Are Deleted e-mails really deleted?"
https://askleo.com/are_deleted_emails_really_deleted/
26. Kadansky Consulting, Inc., 2016. *The Best and Worst Places to Store Your Passwords – Are Yours Secure?*
http://www.kadansky.com/files/newsletters/2016/2016_11_30.html
27. Child Development Institute (2016) *Kid Control: The Secrets Behind Getting it Back and Making it Work.*
https://childdevelopmentinfo.com/how-to-be-a-parent/parenting/parental-control/#gs.0xx9xv
28. Security Baron. 2019 *How to Delete your Social Media Accounts.*
https://securitybaron.com/blog/how-to-delete-your-social-media-accounts/
29. Unknown
30. Internet Archive. (2019) Internet Archive Wayback Machine. http://web.archive.org/

ABOUT THE AUTHOR

Natina Thalien - MBA, CFE *(Certified Fraud Examiner)* holds a double Nationality as French/American and is an Administrator on the ACFE (Association of Certified Fraud Examiners) France Board of Directors.

She has roughly 20 years aggregated experience specializing in Forensic Accounting, Global Audits and Investigations, FCPA Compliance, Anti-Corruption, Fraud Risk and Enterprise Risk Management, Anti-Fraud laws, Mergers, Aggregate Spends tracking, Information Security and Privacy, Sarbanes-Oxley/Internal Controls, and records management in the global marketplace.

Natina has personally managed and performed audits in over 63 different countries in Eastern and Western Europe, Latin America, the Middle East, and the Asia Pacific.

In her spare time, she is an advocate speaker to adolescents about Fraud concerning Social Media presence, CyberCrime, internet Hygiene, WebCam Hacking, Identity Theft, Account Fraud, Wi-Fi, and Public Charging Stations, Fake Documents, Career Development and CyberBullying. She provides TEENS with various information about Wellness Programs and Hotlines available to them if they are victims of such instances mentioned above.

Natina has been an influential speaker on Auditing for Fraud and Corruption to audiences in the USA and UAE, which has provided her to learn, improve, and better understand the complexities that arise within this profession.

Contact the author at **natina@thalien.fr**